. . . . what
you don't
know about
your own
backyard.

*The water*

*...board on Stemmons Freeway has been a Dallas favorite since its Pearl Beer days.*

*The annual assembly of Big Tex.*

# HIDDEN DALLAS

.... what you don't know about your own backyard.

by
## KIRK DOOLEY

TAYLOR PUBLISHING COMPANY, DALLAS, TEXAS

Published by
Taylor Publishing Company
1550 West Mockingbird Lane
Dallas, Texas 75235

Library of Congress Cataloging-in-Publication Data
Dooley, Kirk.
    Hidden Dallas.

    1. Dallas (Tex.)—Description—Guide-books.
I. Title.
F394.D213D66  1987      917.64'28120463      87-26729
ISBN 0-87833-582-X
Printed in the United States of America
10 9 8 7 6 5 4 3 2 1

To Clyde and Dorothy,
who have given me a Dallas ranging
from Duluth Street to Highland Park.

## Acknowledgments

First of all, my appreciation goes to Robert Frese, Jr., who initiated this project and deserves much of the credit for it. Thanks also goes to the Taylor Publishing staff who have assisted in this project.

Photographer Ron Evans, designer Constance (Connie) Flowers, copy editor Nancy (Shoop) Caver, research assistant Cindy McCormick and computer technician Robert Crane all went out of their way to help make this book a success. I am indebted to each of the people on this team.

My wife, Charlotte, helped with encouragement and momentum, and my friends and co-workers at Ranch Publishing and Half Court Press have cheered from the sidelines.

# INTRODUCTION

After studying Dallas for several years, I believe I have come to understand how it has developed its personality and reputation, and I've seen how the city has earned as many perceptions as there are points of view.

There are more than enough Dallasites who have never seen anything outside their own particular neighborhoods, and then have branded the entire city as either superficial or wonderful, depending on which side of the bed they got up on that day. Well, there's more to Dallas than this limited point of view.

Dallas doesn't start with Upper Greenville and end with the Dallas Cowboy Cheerleaders. It's not all concrete and glass, freeways and airports. And the people are not cold and stuffy. Maybe just the ones *you've* met.

Open your eyes to another Dallas. Reach out for the fabric and texture of your city. Seek out the people, places, and happenings of a *Hidden Dallas.*

Where does one start? Try these 10 and go from there:

**1. Experience High Tea at the Adolphus.** The timelessness of this Dallas shrine offers a sense of heritage and graciousness found nowhere else in the city.

**2. Run, walk or cycle along White Rock Lake.** An entire Dallas subculture can be found there, along Lawther Drive, at dawn and dusk. You should be found there, too.

**3. Scream at the wrestlers at the Sportatorium.** Pro wrestling is something you have to see to believe and the Sportatorium is an arena you have to see. I'm not kidding.

**4. See the Mustangs at Las Colinas.** One of the most breathtaking works of sculpture in the world. It makes you proud to be a Texan.

**5. Taste the egg rolls at Texaco Lunch Box.** It's on Ross Avenue. Don't ask any questions, just try it. They don't take Texaco credit cards.

**6. Try the Mesquite Rodeo.** Sure, busloads of tourists flock there, but it's the *real thing,* and it's a prerequisite of living in Dallas or Mesquite.

**7. Walk through Kessler Park.** The loveliest neighborhood in Dallas is tucked away in a wooded section of Oak Cliff. Autumn is the best time to try it.

**8. Ride Amtrak to Austin or San Antonio.** Take the train out of Dallas on Saturday afternoon and return the next day. It'll make you wonder why they invented the airplane.

**9. Imagine the 1800s at the Wilson Block.** Located on Swiss Avenue, west of Baylor Hospital, it's a magical restoration project you'll never forget. It's a hidden Dallas jewel. A must-see.

**10. Hear a lecture at the University of Dallas.** One of Dallas' best kept secrets, UD offers Ivy League-quality speakers, usually free to the public. It's quite a stimulating intellectual environment.

No preservatives were added and no maps have been included. This look at Dallas is strictly BYOM (Bring Your Own Mapsco).

In this book, I have not attempted to define *Hidden Dallas.*

Instead, I hope my observations, insights, and recommendations help you expand and enhance your own perceptions of this place we call Dallas.

-- Kirk Dooley
November, 1987

*Central Expressway.*

# NORTH CENTRAL EXPRESSWAY

If you subscribe to the theory that Dallas was founded as a center of transportation, you must wonder who in the hell created North Central Expressway.

Dallas' traditional main north-south artery, laughingly out of date, is home away from home for half of Richardson and all of Plano. Commuters fume while standstill traffic bottlenecks at each ramp. North Central, it seems, has neither social nor mechanical redeeming value except that it boosts radio drive-time ratings into hyperspace.

North Central, legally known as Texas State Highway 75, starts downtown and, before that, comes rambling in from the south (where she is known, of course, as *South Central*). Before the days of Interstate 45, Houston travelers were able to get a candid view of our city's backdoor as Highway 75 linked the two major Texas cities.

1

On the north side of Dallas, this ultra-modern automobile artery has continued its schizophrenic rush hour ambush on motorists with double-lane efficiency.

Two lanes?!

Why did the Great Roadbuilder in His Wisdom allow this to happen to us?

Well, to begin with, he and others who are familiar with the present situation are giggling at Big D (the International City on the Trinity) because not only did we knowingly build North Central Expressway, we also tore up a perfectly good set of railroad tracks to build it where a railroad once ran. And now, in the 1980s, we're crying for commuter tracks along Central.

This city didn't grow to what it is by accident. We've had a history of smart, visionary leaders dating back to the 1800s BV (Before the Village Apartments), and they have made some great decisions for Dallas. Most of them became fabulously wealthy themselves in the process - and there's nothing wrong with that. But let's stay on the subject. Strong leadership. Civic advancement. Growth. And more growth.

Back when Dallas was a kid, Fort Worth was the cattle capital, Jefferson was the most important city in North Texas and little Dallas wanted to be big. Back in those days, if you weren't on a navigable river or some sort of ancient Spanish Camino Real (trans-Texas trails dating back to

*Changing the HT&C right-of-way to Central Boulevard.*

2

the 1600s), you were in the backwoods and would stay there until they invented Greyhound.

Farmers could grow enough cotton to fill a stadium, but if they couldn't get it to the marketplace, all they had was a Cotton Bowl full of worthless Texas cotton. Transportation was *essential* for this town to get anywhere, and we had two choices: float something down the Trinity River or get one of those new railroads up here.

The former has become a joke for invading hordes of contemporary Dallas visitors, but it wasn't funny in 1867.

Back in the 1860s Dallas leaders tried to build a series of locks and dams between Dallas and the Gulf of Mexico. (You can rent yourself a raft and float a few miles past downtown Dallas and see the haunting Stonehenge-like remnants of some of the locks. They're *in* Dallas County, but they are on private property.)

Of the better known Civil War heroes hailing from Texas, Dick Dowling, the legendary leader of the Battle of Sabine Pass, was hired to try to pilot a ship from the Gulf Coast to Dallas, up the Trinity River. Impossible.

But wait. He could do it! Dowling was the key figure in what Confederate President Jefferson Davis would call "the greatest military victory in the world." (Personally, I think it's actually a toss-up between the Battle of San Jacinto and the 1973 Super Bowl in Miami, when the Cowboys

4

crushed the Dolphins.)

Let's set the stage for the 1863 Battle of Sabine Pass. During the Civil War, the Yankees decided to invade Texas - believe it or not - and cut it off from the rest of the Confederacy. It was a combined sea and land operation under General Nathaniel P. Banks and Admiral David Farragut.

Four thousand Federal troops boarded 17 transports at New Orleans, and, protected by four gunboats, set sail for Sabine Pass, which is where Texas, Louisiana, and the Gulf of Mexico all come together.

And at Sabine Pass, waiting for Farragut, was Dick Dowling.

Farragut had 4,000 men. Dowling had 46. With six small cannons, those 46 men overwhelmed the attackers. Dowling sank one Union gunboat, then waited for a transport with 500 men on board to get within a couple hundred yards, then - boom - sank the transport with one shot.

The fighting lasted less than one hour. The Federal losses included two gunboats, 19 dead, nine wounded, 37 missing, and 350 prisoners. Texas losses: Zero. Nobody killed, nobody wounded. Nobody missing. No runs, no hits, no errors. Nobody left on base.

The incredible victory took a huge chunk out of the Northern morale; it caused a temporary stock drop in New York City and reduced the United States credit abroad by a reported five percent.

But what does Dick Dowling have to do with Dallas, you may ask.

First of all, it needs to be pointed out that he was the Roger Staubach of his time. And secondly, since he was almost beyond mortal, he was the *only* man who could do what no man had ever done - maneuver a ship up the Trinity to the Port of Dallas.

It made no difference to the people of Dallas and Kaufman Counties, who were willing to pay Dowling a whopping $15,000, that Dowling was a war hero and *not* a barge driver.

But Dowling grabbed Captain James H. McGarvey, who *did* know river boat driving, and together, in May, 1867, they departed Galveston in a 60-foot steam wheeler called *Job Boat Number One*.

Unfortunately, they were on the North Central Expressway of rivers. Every few feet they had to push off a sandbar or chop some low-lying branches. Exactly one year and four days later, they pulled up to the side of Dallas, and you would have thought they'd brought Mardi Gras with them. People went bonkers.

The local newspaper, the *Herald,* proclaimed it "the greatest event that will ever occur in the history of Dallas," which may be the first documented evidence of Texas overstatement.

Dowling and McGarvey collected their cash and disappeared. Dallas leaders patted each other on the back and started counting their chickens. They pooled some money and started building Dallas' own steamboat, the *Sallie Haynes,* named for merchant John Haynes' daughter. It was, of course, larger than *Job Boat Number One,* which was on par for the Texas predisposition to outdo the other guy. In this case, however, it was a dumb mistake.

On December 15, 1868, the *Sallie Haynes* left Dallas with tremendous fanfare. Several miles away it met something nobody ever considered - another steamer. Since neither one could pass, they did the most logical thing and exchanged cargo and backed up. Not too long after that, the *Sallie Haynes* hit a stump and sank. And with it sank the hopes of using the upper Trinity for transporting goods.

The good leaders of Dallas, who felt they had some momentum going, continued to press forward. But all their pressing suddenly was directed to the railroad and how *it* would determine the fate of the city.

The Houston and Texas Central Railroad was inching its way north out of Houston. Rumors of an east-west railroad were also being tossed around. The local newspaper put two and two together and reported how getting *both* railroads would mean Dallas would be the transportation hub of North Texas, from the 1870s on into the future.

But at the time, Dallas was no more important

than any other small hamlet in the region. When the H&TC surveyors proposed the route, it missed Dallas by eight miles.

So Dallas tried again. "What will it take?" They pleaded, negotiated, begged and reached into their pockets. They pulled out cash. They pulled out land for a depot. They pulled out all the right-of-way the H&TC had asked for. The city voted 167-11 to give the H&TC what they wanted.

And the ultimate result is your Central Expressway.

Dallas gave the railroad 115 acres of land, free right-of-way through the city, and $5,000 in cash. They got their north-south railroad.

On July 16, 1872, the H&TC chugged into town. Dallas had a population of about 1,000, and over 5,000 people on hand that day from all over North Texas saw the first train pull in along the line that would later become Central Expressway.

While the masses celebrated, the crafty city leaders schemed and plotted how they would lure the transcontinental Texas and Pacific to town. They knew, everyone knew, that whatever town on the H&TC route was also the cross town for the T&P route would become the dominant, peerless city of North Texas.

Our man of the era was John W. Lane. He was a former mayor of Dallas and co-publisher of the *Herald*. At the time, he was our state represen-

*Pulling up the tracks to make way for Central.*

tative in Austin, and it was Senator Lee who quietly added a rider to a bill concerning grants to the railroad that required the T&P to cross the H&TC within one mile of Browder Springs. Nobody cared because nobody knew where it was. When the T&P discovered that by state law they must cross within a mile of Browder Springs, they found out where it was.

It was right next to Dallas.

O.K. Alright, so you Dallas people are sneaky. That was a clever little move. What we'll do is obey the law and move the railroad a mile on the *other* side of Browder Springs (now the site of Old City Park, near downtown).

Now that all other towns were out of the competition, city fathers went back to work and hammered out a deal with T&P - free right-of-way and $100,000 cash if the T&P would pass within 1,200 feet of the town square. The city held an election, and the vote was 192-0 in favor. How many city elections anywhere, anytime, can you name which have been won by unanimous vote?

In August 1873 workmen laid the tracks down Burleson Avenue, and city officials promptly renamed the street Pacific Avenue.

One day while you're drinking, carousing, or just witnessing the drinking and carousing down at the West End, walk over to Pacific Avenue and check out the rusted remains of rail lines just west of Lamar. As you trip over the exposed rails, don't cuss them out. Remember that if it

Old City Park, Dallas' first park.

weren't for the blessed rail lines down that street, you'd be out drinking in a sleepy little ghost town called Dallas.

11

*WARNING:*

*North Central Expressway should be avoided at all costs during the afternoon rush hour.*

If it is unavoidable and you find yourself stranded on Texas' largest parking lot, you'll have ample spare time to enjoy some of the interesting sites along the road.

As you come out of downtown, there is an unusual triangular building where Commerce and Wood Street intersect with Central. That building has been for sale for years. But back in its heyday, back in the early '60s, it was home to one of the most important radio stations of all time: KLIF.

As an intimidating sign on the first level parking area would scream, "NEWS TRUCKS ONLY! NO PARKING!," the actual offices and studio were up on the second level, where the disc jockeys would watch the city below them come and go, like a rising and falling tide in a sea of automobiles.

Owned by Gordon McClendon, "the Old Scotsman," KLIF-AM was a trend setter in American contemporary radio. The station originated the Top-40 radio format, imitated by virtually every radio market in America, and many internationally.

When the Beatles came to Dallas in 1963, KLIF was host station and led the wave of Beatlemania as a generation of Dallasites saw their musical lives change forever.

# ... WELCOME T

While in town during that concert - their only appearance in Dallas as a group - they stayed at what was then the swankiest hotel in town, the Cabana. Later called the DuPont Plaza, it was recently purchased by the county to be used as a jail. (We wonder which car thief will be able to tell his kids he stayed in the "Ringo Starr Suite.")

The Beatles sold out Memorial Auditorium, now part of the Dallas Convention Center, and one front row concert-goer remembers the event as "so many screaming girls we rarely heard the music."

When another British Invasion group, Herman's Hermits, hit Dallas in the mid-'60s, KLIF and its staff hosted them and later found their call letters bannered on a poster on a Herman's Hermits album sold worldwide. The lead singer, Peter Noone (Herman), returned to Dallas on New Year's Eve 1985 as the lead performer at a huge downtown free concert celebrating the beginning of the Texas Sesquicentennial, the state's 150th anniversary.

The top KLIF personality, Irving Harrigan,

# DALLAS . . . .

later left the station when the FM stereo boom took the wind out of AM stations, and he went on to continued success as the most legendary of all Dallas radio personalities in history. More on him when we continue north on Central.

At Pacific Avenue we find a square, tinted glass building, which many architects and most downtown folks would like to see "re-skinned" or painted or *something*. It keeps winning awards for being the ugliest building in Dallas. Formerly, it was the Blue Cross and Blue Shield Building, which had a huge lighted message board bannered across its north face, and for years it flashed a well-known message to southbound motorists, "WELCOME TO DALLAS . . . CITY OF EXCELLENCE."

But the building itself wasn't as significant as the fact that Blue Cross and Blue Shield, one of the most important insurance breakthroughs of its time, was created and founded right here in Dallas.

Just on the other side of the Julius Schepps Freeway (the downtown overpass) is the old Adams Hat Factory at the corner of Canton and

15

Henry.

In 1913 Henry Ford built that building in order to move his Dallas Ford plant from a smaller location on Commerce across from the Dallas Hilton. The original Ford plant in town took roots in December of 1909 when Ford, who had been in business for only six years, came to Texas to expand his horseless carriage enterprise. He set up a two-man sales and service center and had to quickly expand it seven-fold. By 1913 Fords were actually being assembled at that location on Commerce.

Back in those days there were literally hundreds of small manufacturers of cars, but only the best survived, including, of course, Henry Ford.

By 1925 Ford had outgrown its Canton street plant and built a new one on East Grand, which featured the capabilities of assembling 350 cars and trucks per day. Over 100,000 military trucks and jeeps were built there during World War II. The longtime popular slogan at the plant was "Built in Texas by Texans," which was seen by millions as prominent stickers on the back windshields of thousands of locally-built Fords.

By the mid-'60s over 3,000,000 Fords were built in Dallas, and most of them are on North Central at any given moment.

While we're still at the corner of Central and Pacific, we need to stop and realize how that intersection is one of the most important intersections in the state of Texas. When the H&TC Railroad (Central) was crossed by the T&P Railroad (Pacific), that intersection became the center of commerce for all of north Texas. It shifted Dallas from being another small hamlet to being the city which would go on to become one of the important urban areas of the world. Without the intersection of Central and Pacific, there would be no Dallas Cowboys, no EDS, no Fair Park, no Market Center as we know it today. All of those by-products of an aggressive trade center would be in north Texas, but they would exist in Fort Worth or Sherman or Kaufman or Jefferson. Dallas, without the confluence of the two railroads, would probably today be the size of Terrell or Midlothian or Denton, at the most.

Today the great Union Depot is gone from the intersection of Central and Pacific. The massive structure was demolished in 1935. The tracks of the Texas and Pacific were removed in the late '40s. Today, only a memory remains at that site.

Dallas' other grand railroad structure of the era, the Missouri, Kansas, and Texas Railroad (KATY) passenger depot at the corner of Pacific and Market, was torn down in 1924 to build the Interstate Trinity Warehouse, which was recently redeveloped by SPG International as an office building.

Another page in the history of transportation in

Dallas was the death of Gene Goss in the summer of 1984. "Goss on Ross," the most creative and flamboyant used car salesman in the history of this town, once held court on the corner of Central and Ross. The expansion of the freeway caused him to move several blocks east, where the "mayor of Ross Avenue" became a legend in his own time, especially with new and used car dealers.

He was the ultimate trader and could have made a fortune in the advertising business, but he knew there was a huge market most car dealers would rather do without - the "note" business. This clientele usually cannot buy a new car and needs a used car, in its least expensive form, in order to get to work. It's a transient customer who many times quits making payments for whatever reasons and loses the car back to the dealer. It's not a pretty business.

But Goss would make deals with people that established him as the "king of the note lots." He was the dealer's dealer. He had "Go to Work" cars for $49 down. He had "Start to Work" cars - $35 down. And he had "Go to Work Slow" cars for $19 down. One car had a sign, "Runs like Earl Campbell! Guaranteed 10 yards."

His favorite slogan summed up his success. "If you think our cars are bad, ask a hitch-hiker." Clipping from his old classified ads you can find classics. "Buy this '41 Chevy for $595 and get a

'31 Chevy for 1¢. Runs good. Makes good fishin' car."

His trading reputation came from ads like "Would like to trade one of my good clean cars for cement work, carpenter work, musical instruments, tools, guns, horses, mules, or anything worth a few bucks. Goss on Ross."

Over the years he traded cars for such items as a wooden leg, false teeth, a casket, an alligator, a small carnival, and a rollaway bed.

On any given day you would be able to find Goss sitting out on the front porch of his car lot talking with Darrell Royal or Larry Gatlin or any number of celebrities who would drive their tour buses over to Ross Avenue to have an audience with the mayor. Goss was one of the better story tellers of his time in Dallas.

Upon his death in 1984, his wife, Betty, carried on the thriving business with help from her family. Goss' sons took the Goss ingenuity to Austin where their County Line restaurant has become a multi-million dollar chain with locations in several states. It's another testament to the Texas enterprising spirit.

Travelling north on Central, you'll pass the Woodall Rogers Freeway on your left and the Roseland Projects on your right. Woodall Rogers was the mayor of Dallas who fought and scratched for "an ultra-modern automobile highway" which, of course, is Central Expressway.

*The Dallas Hose and Chemical Company #2, near downtown.*

*Proposed CITYPLACE Towers.*

The enormous city within a city being developed by the Southland Corporation, CITY-PLACE, has plans of actually spanning Central Expressway with an above-traffic walkway connecting two 40-plus story skyscrapers. In order to buy the land to pursue the development of CI-TYPLACE, Southland used representatives under dozens of different names to buy individual lots and deterioriating frame houses. When word finally got out that it was the convenience store giant buying up the land, prices went into orbit, and Southland was forced to re-think some of its plans. The great real estate recession of 1986-87 also played a major role in postponing what will ultimately be the City of Dallas' most ambitious mixed-use development ever.

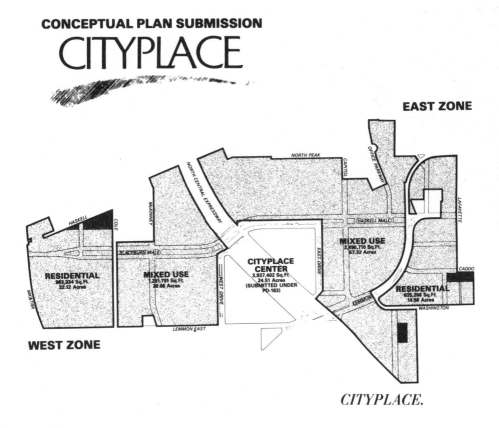

*CITYPLACE.*

Back in the late 1940s and early 1950s the most ambitious development for Dallas was the building of Central Expressway. First mentioned in the 1911 Kessler Plan, "Central Boulevard" was the top recommendation of the 1927 Ulrickson Plan. On October 8, 1937, the State Highway Commission ordered the state highway engineer to make location surveys and prepare right-of-way maps and deeds for a proposed Central Expressway. The $450,000 in bonds voted on during the Ulrickson days didn't seem to be enough money after inflation, the War, and years of talking and planning, and rising construction costs bumped the price to the neighborhood of $20,000,000. But with the City of Dallas providing the right-of-way, the construction costs were handled by city, state, and federal governments.

When construction began in January 1947, the *Dallas Times Herald* said, "Few, if any other roadways, will compare with this modern thoroughfare. It's right-of-way is more than 200 feet in width and will include a three-mile stretch from Bryan to Mockingbird, with 10 traffic lanes - a six-lane expressway designated for 50 miles-per-hour speed, and two service streets on either side from which traffic may enter the expressway at several block intervals. This north-south expressway, spanning from city limit to city limit (10.21 miles) will allow motorists a 'straight shoot' through Dallas."

Unlike many of the newer super-highways in

Dallas, Central Expressway has a "Heinz 57" assortment of commercial enterprises along the access roads. This is because when the H&TC Railroad was changed into central Boulevard, and then into Central Expressway, there was already a standard railroad mix of adjacent commercial and residential buildings.

And it was not a pretty site.

When a railroad would come to town, it would make money transporting goods, but it also made a fortune on the land given to it by eager cities along the route. This was indeed the heart and soul of the Texas real estate business for many years. But when the railroad developed or sold the land along the tracks, the least expensive land, of course, was immediately adjacent to the tracks. In more industrial areas this land was perfect for warehouse districts, such as Deep Ellum, but in a more residential area, cheap, wooden frame houses were constructed along the route. Railroad workers, sporting women, and transient hangers-on were among those who stayed in these inexpensive, sub-standard houses.

A few years ago Central was lined with the remnants of these shanties. But as land prices soared, owners continued to cash out, and office buildings now stand where homes once thrived along the H&TC. For a peek at one of the last remaining pockets of these homes, take Knox St. going west, then turn right on Travis. You'll find the few remaining homes of the maids, cooks,

27

*Mrs. Baird's Bakery offers the best scent in town.*

butlers, and gardeners for the Highland Park homeowners - just across the Missouri, Kansas, and Texas Railroad tracks. The site of the once-grand Highland Park Train Station can be traced by walking a few hundred feet north of the MKT tracks starting at the Knox Street intersection. Part of the cement ramp adjacent to the tracks is still visible today.

Where Central intersects Mockingbird, Mrs. Baird's Bread has positioned its massive bakery as a Dallas institution. The pleasant aroma of the baking bread can be enjoyed throughout the area, including the SMU campus. Tours of the plant are available, and samples of freshly baked bread are nothing short of heavenly. Experiencing the bakery is a *must* for Dallasites of all ages.

The Capital Bank Building, across the intersection from the bakery, houses, among other businesses, radio station KVIL, one of the most successful - if not *the* most successful - radio stations in America. A major reason for its popularity, and hence its financial triumphs, is its morning personality, Ron Chapman. The bearded Chapman was the same disc jockey of 20 years before known as Irving Harrigan, the top KLIF radio man whom we discussed back at the intersection of Commerce and Central. Chapman moved a few miles north on Central Expressway and a few notches up on the radio dial. His constant top ratings and his contribution to Dallas (and Texas) radio have earned him the distinction of being the undisputed king of Dallas radio among his peers in this area and across the nation, where KVIL is at times the most profitable radio station on the air.

A few hundred feet north of Mockingbird is Caroline Rose Hunt's office building known as Premier Place, one of the newer and larger office buildings along the expressway. She is the same woman who developed The Mansion on Turtle Creek, the Crescent, and several other prestigious hotels across the United States. A daughter of H.L. Hunt, she is one of the Grand Dames of Dallas, as well as Texas, in both society and business circles.

At the same location, one of the more popular bowling alleys in North Dallas, Expressway Lanes, used to stay open 24 hours a day. It was demolished to make room for the new office building, and loyal bowlers from SMU and North and East Dallas had to settle for the new state-of-the-art Don Carter Lanes at Northwest Highway and Skillman.

At the corner of Yale and Central, the 6116 Central Exressway building stands remodeled and proud of its heritage as the one-time headquarters of the Dallas Cowboys. Ticket sales, front office headquarters and, in later years, the Dallas Cowboy Cheerleaders made the building their home. As the popularity of the team soared, so did the building's notoriety. It was known simply as "the Cowboy Building."

The best story which can be retold about the Cowboy Building took place during the Cowboys' glory years under the field generalship of Roger Staubach. At one point, the star quarterback wanted an audience with club president Tex Schramm, but the chief was on the phone and Staubach had to wait. He got tired of waiting and finally managed - much to the shock of the Cowboy receptionist - to sneak outside the building and walk along the ledge of the building's top floor and surprise Schramm.

When he got to Schramm's window, the club president's eyes almost popped out at the sight of his bread and butter standing about a foot away from falling to his final quarterback sack.

Staubach got his appointment. Schramm almost had a heart attack. The Cowboys since have moved to Valley Ranch, but many people still refer to the Robert Folsom-owned building as the Cowboy Building.

There are not many landmarks along this stretch of highway, but one was made a couple of

*The neon Big Tex on North Central Expressway.*

years ago when a strong wind toppled the large neon statue of Big Tex at the Centennial Liquor store at Lovers Lane and Central. Letters and phone calls poured in from everywhere, and the Centennial folks paid an arm and a leg to restore and re-stand the giant sign, which has been greeting Central Expressway motorists for years.

*Upper Greenville.*

That same intersection is now known as the gateway for Dallas nightlife along Greenville Avenue. Tourists, conventioneers, Dallasites, and SMU students all contribute to the coffers of the hundreds of bars, shops, and restaurants along Greenville Avenue, starting at Ross and ending at Meadow. But the strip between Lovers Lane and Southwestern has always been the nucleus of the after-hours action.

Thousands of Greenville Avenue funseekers frequent the area every night, but few people realize what brought about that pendulum swing, making Greenville Avenue the top attraction in the city.

Actually it was the effort of two people, Lou and Ann Bovis, back before WWII. The Bovises had a popular nightclub located practically out in the country, at what is now the southeast corner of Lovers Lane and Greenville. The club was called LouAnn's. After Lou's death in the early '50s, Ann continued to run the club which featured dancing to the Big Band sound - the most popular music of postwar America. At LouAnn's large bandstands many of the country's greats - Glenn Miller, Harry James, Tommy Dorsey, Benny Goodman, et al. - played when they hit Dallas. LouAnn's personified the best face Dallas had to offer in the '50s. Where now there are hundreds of choices for dancing in Dallas, back then there was, in many people's opinion, just one. LouAnn's.

Although it is amazing to think that one club could create a path that hundreds of clubs, millions of customers, and billions of dollars have followed, such is the case with LouAnn's. A fire destroyed it in the '60s, and its doors were closed forever, although a smaller club did use the name for a short period.

Ann Bovis leased the now-valuable land for 99 years and retired to a farm near Pilot Point. During LouAnn's heyday, Ann and her family lived on a farm between Fisher and Northwest Highway, west of the Standard Pacific tracks, on what is now Lovers Lane, across from Keller's on Northwest Highway. The Bovises developed some duplexes and sold the rest of their farm.

The land where LouAnn's once stood was divided, and several clubs now stand where the gigantic outdoor patio used to hold hundreds of dancers and partygoers, while thousands more could dance in the three indoor party rooms.

There wasn't anything like LouAnn's during the war years, or post war years, which survived the end of the Big Band Era, and there has never been anything like it in Dallas since. The legacy LouAnn's left behind is the nightlife which followed its lead along thriving Greenville Avenue each night, every year since.

There were, of course, other clubs, such as the Plantation, which had outdoor dancing. The Plantation was located, ironically, near the present site of Cardinal Puff's, currently one of the three or four best known beer gardens in Texas.

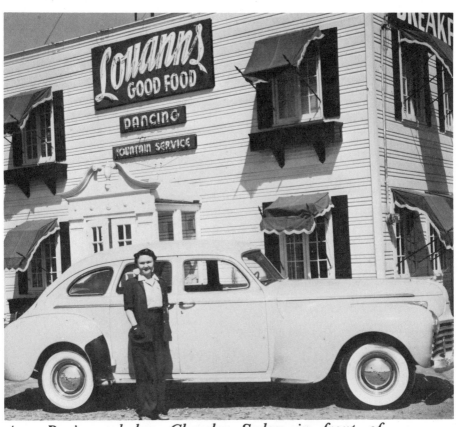

*Ann Bovis and her Chrysler Sedan in front of LouAnn's.*

Hardy's "Pitch and Putt" and a horse riding stable were the thriving businesses which have become the location for one of America's larger apartment complexes: The Village Apartments.

Now the area features a Tom Thumb Supermarket which has evolved into a 24-hour singles paradise, a huge nightclub turned Sound Warehouse and a huge warehouse turned mega-Sigel's liquor store.

Mariano's Restaurant and Cantina was perhaps the most influential restaurant in Dallas when margaritas became the classic southwestern drink. Mariano's also pioneered supreme nachos and sizzling fajitas, two Mexican food fads which, like the margarita, never ended.

*Mariano Martinez and his Dmitri Vail portrait.*

*Helen Dallinger gives curb service to an airplane which landed on Greenville Avenue in 1946.*

For several years during the '60s and '70s Mariano's was recognized as the number one restaurant in America for the sales of margaritas. It was Mariano Martinez who popularized the notion of using a "Slurpee" machine to dispense frozen margaritas. It, also, is now an industry standard. Martinez took his frozen margarita idea a step further and introduced his "Mariano's Margarita Mix," which is sold in stores nationwide. Keep it in the freezer and add tequila. Martinez now makes more money selling his mix than he does in his prime line of work, restauranting.

Leaving Greenville and moving back to Central Expressway, at Caruth Haven you notice a dead-end to the west. Actually, the road could serve as the driveway for the historic Caruth Homeplace, built in 1875.

William Caruth and his brother Walter came to Dallas from Scottsville, Kentucky, about 1850. They opened a store on the banks of the Trinity when Dallas had less than 20 residents. Business was good for "W. Caruth and Bro.," and the two took their profits and began buying rich cotton land north of town.

If you can believe it, the Caruth brothers owned virtually all the land north of Ross Avenue all the way to an area near NorthPark Shopping Mall, between Inwood Road and Abrams. They paid $5 to $10 per acre for over 30,000 acres in what is now among the most expensive tracts of land in the southwest United States.

William built the mansion which still stands on the southwest corner of Northwest Highway and Central Expressway. It is known as "The Caruth Homeplace," and has been a point of interest at that corner for decades as development grew around it and north to . . . well, it changes each month.

Recently, however, the land has been subdivided, and high-priced homes are springing up like a mini-Plano. The home, the acres around it, and the horse stables may soon be nothing more than another North Dallas neighborhood.

That's better than Walter Caruth's home fared. Ten years after brother William built the 1875 home way out in the country, Walter built himself a Victorian mansion closer to town, at what is the present-day intersection of Greenville and Belmont. His home was a beautiful structure, but he sold it four years later when he realized a 7000% profit for selling it and the 170 acres around it for $117,800 in 1889.

*Aerial view of Northwest Highway, looking west.*

*Aerial view of NorthPark during its 1965 opening.*

The Crash of 1893 bankrupted August Belmont, the new owner of the property, and it wasn't until 1919 that the Caruth mansion was sold to Miss Ela Hockaday who turned the home into the Hockaday School for Girls.

In 1961 Hockaday moved to its present location in North Dallas, and in 1962 the school building, named "Bosque Bonita" by Caruth in 1885, was demolished to make way for an apartment development which still stands today.

Across from the Caruth homestead along Central is the NorthPark Shopping Mall, a Raymond Nasher development which set a new standard for shopping in Dallas and to this day is one of the more popular shopping areas in North Texas. Its key was to lure Neiman-Marcus from its first suburban location in Preston Center.

The standard of excellence which NorthPark set has been emulated by Valley View, Galleria, Prestonwood and other high-class shopping malls in the Dallas area, but none reflects the importance of art like NorthPark. Nasher has always believed in combining business and art, and many feel this is why NorthPark remains as popular today as it was when it opened.

At one point during NorthPark's early days, WFAA-TV had a remote studio in one of the storefronts. There it filmed a locally-produced teen dance show called "Sumpin' Else," featuring local high school students as dancers. The show was hosted by Ron Chapman, who as we

*NorthPark at night.*

now know, worked at Central and Commerce at KLIF, and still works at Central and Mockingbird at KVIL. The most popular dancer during this mid-'60s teen beat era was Miss Teenage Dallas, Joanie Prather, grandaughter of Hugh Prather, Sr., who developed Highland Park 50 years before.

NorthPark gained further notoriety in 1986 when rock star David Byrne, leader of the band "Talking Heads," filmed his movie "True Stories" at NorthPark.

Few people realize the NorthPark parking lot served as the site of the early "Starfest" concerts, which initiated in 1975 with 13 concerts. At that time it was called "Summertop" and has proven to be enormously successful as it matured at the Park Central location a few miles north on North Central Expressway. An announcement in mid-1987 by the Dallas Symphony Association disclosed a plan to play at a permanent site being built by the Pace Concert people in Carrollton.

The first Summertop season was headlined by Willie Nelson, who was just beginning to make a name for himself as an Austin-based "progressive music" outlaw. Country and Western music had always been headquartered in Nashville. Nelson, as a crew-cut, shy songwriter, never made it as an entertainer in the hard-line Nashville style. Some of his songs, like "Crazy," a hit by Patsy Cline, and "Hello Walls," a hit by Ray Price, helped Nelson make a comfortable living as a

46

Tennessee songwriter. But his heart was in entertaining, and Nashville didn't allow him to wander from its narrow parameters.

When Nelson's home in Tennessee burned down, he had all of that confinement he could take. He came home to Texas (he had been born in Abbott, right on I-35, south of Dallas) and headed straight for the state capital. Together with other Nashville "outlaws" such as Waylon Jennings (who's only claim to fame at the time was that he was Buddy Holly's bass player on the tour when Holly died), Nelson began experimenting with a new country sound that had more of a rock influence.

Willie and Waylon and the boys, such as Dallasites Michael Murphey, Ray Wylie Hubbard, B.W. Stevenson, and Willis Alan Ramsey, helped create a whole new American sound - the Austin sound - which revolutionized hard-line country music and helped spawn southern rock. New Yorker Jerry Jeff Walker, Texan Rusty Wier, and Bosque County native Steve Fromholz rounded out the top Texas talents who used the now-demolished Armadillo World Headquarters as a spiritual haven for their new music.

It was Fromholz who was the leading headliner at Dallas' second Summertop concert series during the Bicentennial summer of 1976, which featured 34 events, more than doubling the 13 from the first year.

Hundreds of thousands attend today's series

*Summertop at NorthPark.*

called "Starfest," but few would know that the beautiful outdoor concert series had been simply a big blue-and-white tent set up on the North-Park parking lot where Fuddrucker's now stands.

Just north of NorthPark, the exclusive Glen Lakes residential development stands, bordered on the north by Walnut Hill. To some it is the nicest, safest neighborhood in Dallas. Vacant lots sell for about $1 million each. But to others, mostly oldtimers, they remember Glen Lakes as one of the prettier golf clubs in the city. The 18 holes are now homes, apartments, retail, and a large office building, just east of Central.

At the northeast corner of the intersection of Central and Walnut Hill is a Centennial Liquor store which became famous as the top-selling liquor store in Dallas. Those who enjoy a sip of beer, wine or liquor know that everything north of that store is a "dry" area, all the way to the city limits and beyond.

Just north of Royal Lane, on the east side of Central Expressway, is a building known only by its sign, "Stewart Company," and its eye-catching, avant-garde mosaic art covering the entire front of the building, which was built about the time Central Expressway was constructed.

What is that piece of art? What is it called? What does it mean? Why has it inspired some and confused other commuters for over 30 years?

The mural is called "Genesis," and was created by Mexican artist/archaeologist/writer Miguel Covarrubias in 1955. It is the story of the creation as seen by the ancient peoples of America. The powers of the universe shown are based on the Indian concept of the four elements: water, earth, fire and air (or sky).

"Genesis" is probably the most visible, most intriguing and least understood of Dallas' art resting in public places. To fully grasp the mosaic, pull off North Central onto the service road one day, park safely off the roadway and read how the creator of "Genesis" describes the work:

"Water is represented by a blue whirlpool with

*The "Genesis" mural at the Stewart Company on North Central Expressway.*

fishes and other water animals. On the left, the Moon, with a face in the style of the Hopi Indians, peers out of the night. Next is the Rain, dripping out of a large, dark cloud made of serpentine shapes that suggest the mask of the Rain-god. Further to the right is the personified Rainbow, also in the style of the Southwest, who functions as a messenger between Heaven and Earth. He wears a turquoise mask and a precious feather on his head. The Earth is a dark cave, home of *Tlaltecuhtli*, 'Lord of the Earth,' a monster, half jaguar, half alligator. On the Earth's surface grow some of the plants of Texas and a native Indian plant, a sunflower.

"Fire is represented by a burst of flames which is vaguely reminiscent of a serpent's or dragon's head. Above, among the smoke, is a great hand, representing the power of God in creating the plants of the field before they were in the earth, also all intelligence and science. It has a live oak acorn, 'the gift of life.' Next is the Sun, the 'Giver of Life, which, like the Moon, has a face in the style of the Southwest. Finally, on the extreme right, is the Air or the Sky, represented by a rather abstract shape, a spiked spiral, taken from a section of a large conch shell, which was the symbol of *Quetzalcoatl*, the ancient Mexican sky god, who represented the positive, creative forces of nature. His symbol is surrounded by sky elements, the constellations and the birds.

"The symbols and the style for these come

from the pictorial manuscripts of the Mixtecs of Southern Mexico, roughly dated between the 12th and 13th century.

"The ancient inhabitants of America were peoples of all sorts: there were barbaric, warlike tribes, as well as highly civilized nations of priests and statesmen, artists and scientists, who built great cities, cultivated astronomy and mathematics, and left us unexcelled examples of their fine taste and great craftsmanship. These civilized peoples, such as the Pueblos of the Southwest, the authors of the culture of Hopewell, the Mayas, Toltecs, Aztecs and the builders of the great civilizations of the Andes, were all intensely religious and ruled their lives and all their actions by a cult of nature: the elements - the Earth and the Sky, Water and Fire, the Sun, the Moon, the Stars and so forth.

"The myth symbolized the eternal struggle between good and evil, and the two aspects, negative and positive, creative and destructive, of the elements of nature. It has some curious points of agreement with our modern scientific belief: their stories of nebulae, of floods and of lands emerging from the sea, of an ice age, a volcanic era and so forth, and they show a keen preoccupation for the understanding and explaining of the mysterious forces of nature."

And you thought it was just a weird painting that meant nothing.

As you continue north on Central and ap-

proach the intersection at the Lyndon B. Johnson
Freeway (I-635), to your right will be the Gemini
Drive-In Theater, owned by the late Gordon
McLendon, the same man who gave you KLIF
and Top 40 radio.

The Gemini has one of the more interesting his-
tories of drive-in theaters in the Southwest. It
was the biggest in the world at one point; it was
the first to include two screens at one site (a look
at any new movie theater in America shows how
innovative McLendon was at the time); and
among other things, a McLendon man from one
of his radio stations, KNUS-FM, once set the
world record for flagpole sitting while thousands
of Central Expressway commuters cheered daily
from the highway.

Just like most other drive-in theaters, the Gemini will someday be sold and developed, leaving
nothing more than a new office building and a
memory.

Before you cross LBJ Freeway, back to your
left is the giant Park Central office complex,
which was formerly a golf course. To your northeast is the international headquarters for Texas
Instruments, one of the most important companies in the history of Dallas, as well as Texas.

It was at Texas Instruments during July of
1958 that a research analyst named Jack S.
Kilby made one of the great discoveries of our

*The Texas Instruments semiconductor plant in 1958.*

*Jack S. Kilby.*

time. His concept, which was successfully tested in September of that same year, was the first step in America's "second industrial revolution."

Kilby created the first integrated circuit (tiny pieces of silicon on which minute electronic circuits are printed), better known today as a chip. The discovery of the chip paved the way for personal computers and thousands of other electronic devices of the computer age.

Bell Laboratories had introduced the transistor in 1948, but this great discovery was frustrating because although engineers could design intricate

A wafer of germanium has been prepared as shown to form a phase shift oscillator.

Plateaus → 

Oot

−V

+V

The bulk resistance of the germanium was used for resistor, and a p-n junction for a capacitor. The p type Ge wafer was diffused by conventional technique, and an aluminum emitter dot was evaporated & alloyed. Gold was evaporated and alloyed to provide connections to the transistor base and to the capacitor area. Plateaus were formed by etching for the transistor and capacitor. Tabs were attached to make contact with the Germanium wafer as shown. The wafer was mounted on a glass slide with Sauereisen cement, and gold wires bonded thermally to make the necessary interconnections. The unit was then given a cleanup etch.

When 10 volts were applied (1000 Ω series current limiting resistor), the unit oscillated at about 1.3 Mc, amplitude about 0.2 v pp. This test was witnessed by W. A. Adcock, Bob Pritchard, Mark Shepard, and others.

JS Kilby
September 12, 1958

*Kilby's actual notes on the silicon chip.*

circuits, they were too small to be made by hand - that is, until TI's Kilby made the breakthrough which hundreds were working on all across the nation.

Kilby joined TI in April of 1958 to work on the "tyranny of numbers," as the project was called. The proposed solution was to devise a method to fit components together without wiring.

Kilby worked alone in his office during the month of July because all TI employees took their vacation at the same time. Since he had not worked there long enough to earn his vacation time, he had to work on the tyranny of numbers alone.

He considered silicon. TI already had a silicon transistor. Plus he already knew that parts of regular semiconductor devices, diodes and transistors, could be made of silicon. He continued to ponder silicon.

The idea that one material, silicon, which was doped with the proper impurities to make it conduct an electric current, could be used as a single chip made up of the necessary circuits and components was called the "Monolithic Idea."

On September 12, 1958, Kilby's device was successfully tested at the Texas Instruments laboratories, and the tyranny of numbers was at last conquered, ushering in the computer age.

Kilby and Californian Robert Noyce, who reached a similar conclusion from a different per-

*The site of the Texas Instruments semiconductor facility in 1958.*

spective, both are credited jointly for the Mono-lithic Idea, and both received the National Medal of Science for their works.

Many technological dreams, such as putting a man on the moon, might not have come about without the creation of the silicon chip. And it happened during a lonely July, 30 years ago on the edge of Central Expressway.

# NEIGHBORHOODS

With the exclusion of two irritating real estate recessions, the 1970s and '80s have been a boom for the Dallas real estate business - which is doing nothing more than keeping up with the growth of the city.

The rows of suburban tract and custom homes are endless as Dallas continues to bust at its seams. Nowhere is this more evident than in Plano, which is either paradise or nightmare, depending on whether you are living the "American Dream" in your ultramodern home or you are a homebuilder who got caught in the Crash of 1986. Over 1,000 builders were active in the Plano market when the bottom dropped out of oil and real estate in 1986. Most builders, including the largest independent builder, Mickey Murry, either declared bankruptcy or moved on to the next boom town.

## he Residence Show Place

MUN

OU WANT A HOME—a permanent place of residence for your family
You want a home conveniently located 'midst healthful and comfortabl
surroundings. ¶ You want a location that will always be identified wit
social and commercial life of the city.

You want a home where environments are best—where surrounding influ
es make for the ideal home-life.

You want a home where improvements and conveniences adequately antic
e the future growth and development of the city.

You want a home which has a *permanent* and ever increasing value—one tha
always be classed as typical of the best to be found in the city.

You want a city man's home, that is closely associated with every phase c
life and so located as to benefit from every forward civic movement.

You want a home to be proud of—not a temporary abiding place, but
e that will at once suggest the thought—"There is an *Ideal* Home."

Of all sites in the South, none are more able to supply these requirement
n Munger Place.

d Munger Boulevard

# ER PLACE

### THE CITY MAN'S HOME

## The 'Place for

**M**UNGER PLACE is in itself "A City of Homes." right in the heart of the city — far enough from bu — near enough to be convenient. It is high and co breezes in summer. (*The water main from new White Rock Res through, which will soon supply abundance of pure water at high*

Munger Place is the home of business men who are vitall growth and development of the city.

Munger Place has all streets paved, driveways parked—sh placed with an eye for symmetry—gas, electricity, sewerage, e for *every* residence.

Munger Place is directly in the path of the city's future g

Munger Place is judiciously restricted, where homes are ful, artistic, exclusive.

Munger Place cars run out Elm street from the courtho providing a direct line to the business center, free from dirt ar

Munger Place is *the* ideal home-place; its size, its locatio of its citizenship, forever banish all doubt as to its permanency

The aftermath of the building craze, however, was the presence of several thousand new homes in dozens of subdivisions which sat unoccupied for almost two years. Rows and rows and rows of seemingly identical houses, most of which were built with Chicago Antique brick, were repossessed by banks when the market for them disappeared. Even after slashing prices, the banks found the supply still outweighed the demand.

As the economic trend began to correct itself (as it always does), Plano moved out of one of the most amazing circumstances ever seen in the history of Texas. Entire neighborhoods of sparkling new castles, most of which were in the $250,000-$450,000 price range, sat empty with an endless line-up of "For Sale" signs. It was truly a ghost town of the American Dream.

But with the market back in sync in Plano, we can look back and see how it was nothing more than the latest in a long line of chapters in a volume you could name "The Growing Pains of Dallas."

While newcomers flock to the Planos and Las Colinases and Duncanvilles of the area, they have the option of never leaving their own neighborhoods. The developments of today are so planned out, so all-encompassing, that all your worldly needs are met within five minutes of your home. Although this leads to a better sense of neighborhood, it unfortunately helps alienate Dallasites from their own city.

While no one can argue about the freshness and conveniences of the modern suburban home, neighborhoods made up of these houses are too young to have an established personality and heritage.

Being a part of Dallas should include a broader perspective of the city, its residents and its neighborhoods. And if you don't have that understanding of the heritage of Dallas, here's how to go about starting:

Get in your car, right now, and drive to the Wilson Block.

This will be your starting point for a visual tour of Hidden Dallas. Even if you've lived in the city for years, if you haven't experienced the Wilson Block, you need to do so, posthaste. You'll be

*The Biltmore area of Plano.*

surprised at the richness of the heritage it represents, and it will open your eyes to a Dallas that has nothing to do with malls or freeways or suburbs or the Ewings. The Wilson Block is located on Swiss Avenue, between downtown Dallas and Baylor Medical Center. Swiss runs east-west between Live Oak and Gaston. Just west of Hall Street is the intersection of Swiss and Oak Street. In this unlikely location sits the most spectacular restoration project in Dallas.

Recently, the Meadows Foundation funded the restoration of two blocks of old, turn-of-the-century Queen Anne-style frame homes, which have miraculously survived both the decay and the urban redevelopment in the area.

There, at 2922, majestically stands the *only* remaining survivor of the hundreds of 19th century Victorian mansions which once thrived in the neighborhood. It is now the headquarters for the Meadows Foundation, which is also restoring the smaller carriage houses and other homes on the Wilson Block and the adjoining Beilharz Block. The Meadows Foundation is allowing nonprofit organizations to office in these spectaular homes once they are restored.

Frederick P. Wilson arrived in Dallas in 1872. He and his brother, John, were Canadians who came to Texas to get involved in the cattle business. Within 15 years the brothers were herding Texas longhorn cattle to Wyoming, where they

Home of C. H. Munger

## Your Neighbors

**I**F YOU DESIRE to select your next door neighbors from among your own congenial friends, we will make satisfactory terms and prices, provided you will build immediately desirable residences thereon, and we will be glad to consult with those having that end in view. No lots will be sold for speculation, though we will sell a lot to one who will build immediately and live thereon, with an agreement to hold an adjoining lot for a short time ... ding their securing a desirable r ... urchase, build and live ... on ... ity like this is sel ... d ... n make "your ... ... ctly high- ... ... place.

Home of D. E. Waggoner

## Accessibility

**N**EARLY every street of importance through East Dallas enters Munger Place—Bryan street passes between it and St. Mary's College and has a direct line of street railway into the city with a twelve minute schedule. The place is also bisected by Live Oak street, Swiss avenue, Gaston avenue and Junius street—all giving direct outlets to any part of Dallas' business or residence districts. The property is two miles from the postoffice and about fifteen minutes drive by carriage or ten minutes by motor. Other lines of street railway, which are easy of access, afford quick transportation to any portion of the city. The Dallas-Sherman Interurban also has a park station at Munger Pl...

pastured them for the summer, then shipped them by rail to St. Louis. In 1894 Frederick married Henrietta Frichot, the niece of French La Reunion veteran Jacob Nussbaumer.

Within four years they acquired all of the Nussbaumers' East Dallas property and built the magnificent Queen Anne-style home on the corner of Swiss and Oak, all before the turn of the century. The home was said to be a miniature replica of the Czarina's summer palace in Belorussia.

Wilson also built three rent houses on the property, which are all part of the Meadows' restoration project. The home at 2902, now the headquarters of the Historic Preservation League, was built for Dr. T.E. Arnold, who was pursuaded to immigrate from Geneva, Switzerland, to Dallas in 1891.

Wilson's wife's sister, Laura Beilharz, and her husband, Theodore, built a gambrel-roofed Beilharz home on the block. He was the stonemason who did the exterior work on many Dallas buildings of the era. He, too, was Swiss-born. Their house has since been moved to 4903 Reiger, in the Munger Place Historical District.

More in-depth information of the heritage of the Wilson Block can be obtained there during office hours. But as you gaze at the majestic Wilson home, try to picture *an entire neighborhood* of similar structures. Your image would be a true

*The Wilson Block on Swiss Avenue.*

scenario of that area in the 1890s. And, mournfully, all the homes outside of the Meadows' protective net have been demolished.

Between the Wilson Block and downtown still stands the only other remnant of this early European-based neighborhood, the St. Joseph's German Catholic Church, which survives as a Korean Catholic church. Built in 1910, it still serves its congregation at the corner of Swiss and Texas.

To the south of the Wilson block, evidence along Gaston of the railroad boom remains today. To the west is downtown, to the east is Baylor Hospital and the rest of East Dallas. But just to the north is one of the more interesting redevelopment efforts in modern Dallas history.

69

Bryan Place, looking west.

Bryan Place, once located in the heart of the City of East Dallas, is a new redevelopment effort spearheaded by Dallas builder David Fox, who was president of Fox and Jacobs homebuilders. Bounded roughly by the Central Business District (downtown), Ross Avenue, Live Oak, and Washington, Bryan Place was developed exactly a century after the incorporation of the City of East Dallas, in 1882.

Over the years, urban blight had destroyed this once-thriving neighborhood, and when it became apparent that urban pioneers could not bring it back, an innovative new approach by Fox was enacted. He felt he could recapture the feeling of an older neighborhood with a new development which featured pedestrian-oriented streets and sidewalks, balconies, and tight spacing.

*The Fox and Jacobs development, Bryan Place.*

71

*Fishburn's on Ross Avenue.*

The neighborhood, with virtually all new homes, shares the same older schools and commercial buildings, including the Fishburn's Cleaners plant at 3200 Ross at Pavilion, where they have headquartered since 1913. Part of the movie "A Trip to Bountiful" was filmed there. It was the bus station scene when the character played by Geraldine Page was trying to hide from her son and daughter-in-law while she searched for her hometown of Bountiful, Texas. Ms. Page won the Academy Award for Best Actress for her performance in that film.

Homes in Bryan Place have borrowed floorplans and accouterments from homes in Old East Dallas, including bay windows, lofts, high ceilings, and steeply pitched roofs. The convenience of walking to work downtown has attracted both a "Yuppie" breed as well as newcomers to Dallas who have enjoyed inner city living back east. A homeowners' association has built a community swimming pool and clubhouse and organized several social activities throughout the year.

With the Southland Corporation's CITY-PLACE development just north of Bryan Place, this area will be one of the key residential redevelopment areas in Dallas for the next several years.

Although Bryan Place is an example of a neighborhood going full circle, Dallas does have an excellent example of how caring people made the difference in an area where nothing had to be torn down at all.

It is truly a majestic area, a street which can remind Dallasites of a romantic era of the city. And just before it fell into total decay, it was saved. Because of that, we can all enjoy the magnificence of the Swiss Avenue Historical District.

To get to this area from Bryan Place, go back to the Wilson Block and head east on Swiss Avenue. When you cross Fitzhugh you will enter the Historical District.

Listed as a Texas Historical Site, the Swiss Avenue Historical District is also in the National Register of Historic Places. It is especially important locally because it was the first historical district in Dallas.

Developed as a part of the 1905 Munger Place addition, it was originally advertised as "the most attractive and desirable residence district in the entire Southland."

Swiss Avenue, now considered a separate neighborhood from Munger Place, was different from the beginning. It was ambitious, it was unique and it was more impressive than anything ever seen in Dallas. The two previous affluent sections of Dallas, The Cedars and parts of Ross Avenue, were outmaneuvered by R.S. and Collett Munger. Their new development had built-in deed restrictions which required houses to be two stories, have uniform setbacks from the street, and cost at least $10,000 each. Rigid building requirements demanded that each home be individually designed by an architect, and today you will see Neoclassical, Tudor, Italian Renaissance, Prairie, Spanish Eclectic and Colonial Revival styles of mansions along the live oak-lined boulevard.

This was indeed the most impressive section of Dallas during its time, but as Highland Park came in later and Dallas began to grow north, both Munger Place and Swiss Avenue began to deteriorate.

After World War II, Gaston Avenue and most of Live Oak fell victim to the practice of cutting large homes into several apartments. This was done along Swiss, but the next step, which was to tear down the stately old mansions and build actual apartment buildings (as on Gaston and Live Oak), was prevented when concerned Swiss Avenue homeowners banded together to save the dignity of their neighborhood. That's when the Historical Preservation League was born.

In 1973 a revolving fund was established by the League, which purchased multiple properties in the area from absentee owners, then sold them to homeowners for restoration.

And today, the grandeur of the early 1900s lives again with a new breed of urban pioneers. They are not bothered by the area's crime, ethnic diversity and public schools as much as they

*Swiss Avenue mansion.*

*would be* bothered by the lack of heritage, the traffic nightmares and the *sameness* of a fresh new suburb far from the center of Dallas. To each his own . . .

All aesthetics aside, Swiss Avenue homes which were selling for under $100,000 in 1970 are now over the $400,000 mark. Living in those homes are - once again - some of Dallas' top business, civic and financial leaders.

When you see Swiss Avenue, you should park your car and walk it. No other street in Dallas has its rich heritage. Swiss was named by Jacob Nussbaumer (who you'll recall was part of the La Reunion experiment), who named it for his native country. It was originally called the Old White Rock Road. It was the most impressive street for years, but it suffered decay after WWII and was rezoned for multi-family development in the '60s. Almost lost, it was saved by the people of Dallas and now it thrives again. One of its great ironies is that its proximity to downtown - or its being considered "inner city" - was for years its biggest drawback. Now it is one of its greatest attributes.

Each year on Mother's Day weekend, the second weekend in May, the Swiss Avenue Historic District Association hosts a Tour of Homes. For a small fee, you and thousands of other interested Dallasites can tour selected homes. There're no two ways about it: it's a thrill to see the interiors of the tour homes. Go ahead and mark your cal-

*Jogging along Swiss Avenue.*

endar now. It makes a great Mother's Day gift.

And you may be one of those people who don't like to jog around a track. One Saturday, just take your Reeboks over to Swiss and run in a setting that is as pleasant as they come. It is truly a hidden part of Dallas.

Why were Munger Place and Swiss Avenue successful from the beginning?

Dallas' most prominent citizens appreciated the severe deed restrictions, and they chose to build mansions along Swiss. Railroad magnates, bankers, lawyers, doctors, judges, cotton magnates, and other wealthy citizens became residents of this swank development. It was so magnificent, it was almost timeless.

The largest taxpayer in Texas, Colonel C.C. Slaughter, was among the first to build a home there. He was one of the most fascinating men in Texas. Slaughter was a banker, Texas Ranger, cattleman, philanthropist and one of the most famous ranchers in America.

Born in the early days of the Republic of Texas, Slaughter was a pioneer in West Texas ranching. By the turn of the century he had accumulated more than one million acres of land and over 40,000 head of cattle. His land made up much of the southern half of the Texs panhandle. Newspapers as far away as Dallas were calling him the "Cattle King of Texas" a decade before Texas ranchers hit the "beef bonanza" of the 1880s.

He was among the first to use barbed wire and windmills, and he successfully introduced new cattle breeds to West Texas. In 1899 he shocked the nation when he bought a Hereford bull named Sir Bredwell for an unprecedented $5,000.

He was a large booster of Baylor University and other Baptist causes. In 1890 he served on the building committee of the First Baptist Church in Dallas, the largest Baptist church in the world. The committee supervised the building of the church's sanctuary, which is still used today. Of the total costs - $90,940 - Slaughter donated a reported $60,000.

In May of 1903 his pastor, George Washington Truett, influenced Slaughter to donate the first $50,000 to a new Baptist hospital in Dallas. In March, 1904, the Texas Baptist Memorial Sanitarium opened on a pasture where Slaughter used to work cattle. The little health facility grew, and Slaughter continued to support it financially. It was reported that the directors of the hospital had wanted to honor him by naming the hospital for him but had prudently chosen to call it something besides Slaughter Hospital. In 1920 it was renamed Baylor Hospital, the same hospital where, in March of 1986 (the Texas Sesquicentennial), a young professional wrestler named Mike Von Erich was treated for Toxic Shock Syndrome. His worldwide popularity was so great that while he was at Baylor the main switchboard took an average of 400 calls per hour, 24 hours a day, for two weeks, from well-wishers around the world.

The massive Baylor Medical Center, located in

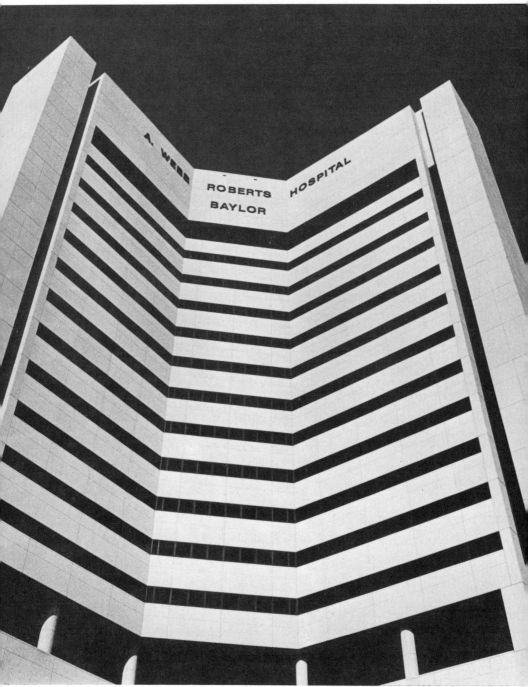

*Baylor Medical Center.*

East Dallas between the Wilson Block, Bryan Place, and the Swiss Avenue Historical District, is today one of the leading hospitals in the Southwest.

Slaughter has left other legacies as well. He was a founder of the Texas Cattle Raisers Association in 1877, and he was a founder of the American National Bank of Dallas in 1884, which through subsequent mergers is now called First RepublicBank Corporation.

Although his family name is not as prominent in Dallas today as it is in West Texas, several of his descendants, especially the ones who found oil on the West Texas land they inherited, are prominent business figures in Dallas. The Browning family, owners of Precision Motors, also invested in the start-up of the Dallas Mavericks. The De-Loache family has invested in several Dallas projects, the most notable being the development of Preston Hollow.

In November of 1939 Preston Hollow (bounded by Northwest Highway, Park Lane, Preston Road and Meadowbrook) was incorporated as a tax-free city. Ira P. DeLoache used his office as City Hall. Today the City Hall of Preston Hollow, Texas, is the Ebby Halliday sales office at Northwest Highway and Preston Road.

Across the street was the O'Connor Dairy, which is now Preston Center.

Preston Hollow was basically split in half by

what is now the Dallas North Tollway, but back then it was the Cotton Belt Railroad. Residents in the area actually commuted downtown, using the Meader Road Station.

In 1945 Dallas annexed the City of Preston Hollow, and these days more than twice the original area is known by the name Preston Hollow.

That little frame house on the corner of Preston Road and Northwest Highway must be magic. Ebby Halliday went from that little office to become one of the most successful Realtors in America. Her little operation, which she started in 1945, grew to be the largest independently owned residential real estate firm in Texas. Besides being the winner of the Easterwood Cup (presented to Dallas' top Realtor), she has also been named the top Realtor in Texas and was president of the Women's Council of the National Board of Realtors.

In the tradition of Sarah Cockrell, Mary Crowley, and Mary Kay Ash, Ebby Halliday has been one of Dallas' top women business leaders. She broke down an important gender door when she became the first female president of the North Dallas Chamber of Commerce.

While Ebby Halliday and company grew to amazing proportions, an interesting comparison would be Douglas Newby. He, too, is a member of the Greater Dallas Board of Realtors - with over 7,000 members now - but Newby is a study

*Douglas Newby, Dallas restoration leader.*

in contrast. While Halliday reflects the dynamic
growth of Dallas, Newby reflects a more special-
ized side of residential real estate in the city - res-
torations. He began small and stays small, but
nobody in Big D has the thorough understanding
of Old East Dallas like Newby.

He has restored many older homes himself and
understands both the emotional as well as the re-
alistic side of restoration projects.

84

Newby works primarily in the Munger Place Historical District, just southwest of the Swiss Avenue Historical District, bordered roughly by Gaston, Columbia, Fitzhugh, and Munger. There are no boulevards like Swiss Avenue, but the homes, as a group, make up an enchanting neighborhood. The houses are known for their symmetry in style: uniform spacing, setbacks and wide front porches on two story frames, usually with Neoclassical or a Dallas version of Prairie-style architecture. Some homes are Craftsman bungalows with broad, overhanging, hipped roofs, and other homes are turn-of-the-century houses which show a Mediterranean influence.

This neighborhood, more than Swiss Avenue, was in horrible shape when a handful of Dallas preservationists accepted the challenge to attempt restoration. Only a few homes were owner occupied, and most had already been subdivided.

Incredibly, these homes were selling for less than their original 1905 prices. The first wave of smart buyers were artists, who came into a bad neighborhood armed with a determination many urban pioneers would have to call courageous. They were completely outnumbered by transient renters, and the area was rough. But the artists were drawn to the neighborhood by the 10- and 12-foot ceilings, large windows and porches and even the severe patchwork fabric of the neighborhood.

Artists are never known for enjoying, doing, or seeing what everyone else does, so moving to Richardson or Plano was never a question for them.

After they established a beachhead, the urban pioneers came in armed with the mandatory political insights necessary to initiate legislation to help them turn Munger Place around.

These young professionals and their Historical District received national attention when the Federal National Mortgage Association selected Munger Place as the national demonstration area for its innovative inner-city lending program.

And as adventuresome urban pioneers completed their various restoration projects in the area, many were surprised when roots began to grow, small children began to appear and the adventure turned into a permanent home. Munger place is once again enjoying the prestige it was created to have over 80 years ago.

The streets to look for are Worth, Junius, Tremont, Victor and Reiger going west from Munger. When you see or hear information about the Old East Dallas Homes Tour, take advantage and see these homes.

Other older neighborhoods in Old East Dallas worth seeing are:

1. Junius Heights (bordered by Gaston, Columbia and Beacon)

2. Belmont (bordered by Greenville, McCommas and Skillman)

3. Greenland Hills (bordered by North Central, McCommas and Greenville)

4. Vickery Place (just south of Greenland Hills)

5. Cochran Heights (bordered by North Central, Henderson and Fitzhugh)

6. Mill Creek (bordered by Gaston, Columbia, Peak and Fitzhugh)

7. Mount Auburn (bordered by Beacon, Glasgow, Sante Fe and Grand)

8. Hollywood Heights (just east of Mount Auburn)

9. Park Estates (bordered by Columbia, Sante Fe, Glasgow and Lakewood County Club)

10. Lakewood (bordered by Abrams, Gaston and White Rock Lake)

And the greatest of these is Lakewood.

*Lakewood Boulevard.*

*Old Lakewood Country Club.*

*Newer view of Lakewood Country Club.*

There are a healthy number of Dallasites who feel Lakewood is the finest neighborhood in all of North Texas. Finer than Highland Park, finer than Bent Tree, finer than Las Colinas or Preston Hollow.

In the 1920s and 1930s it - along with Highland Park - *was* unquestionably the choicest place to live. And the fact that third generation Dallasites are now attending Woodrow Wilson High School is testament that Lakewood boasts the heritage that newer neighbors have yet to acquire.

The Lakewood Country Club, established in 1912, is second only to the Dallas Country Club in longevity. Surrounding the club, an addition by Albert Dines and Lee Kraft called Lakewood Country Club Estates is still considered the most desirable section of Lakewood. Other additions by Dines and Kraft were Gastonwood and Westlake Park.

The English Tudor, French Eclectic, Colonial Revival and especially the Spanish Eclectic architectural styles nestled on oversized wooded lots give Lakewood a coveted look of elegance it has retained over the years.

The best glance at Lakewood can be seen by taking Lakewood Boulevard east from Abrams (right next to the newly renovated Lakewood Shopping center). Along Lakewood Boulevard take note of extensive use of stained glass, Spanish tile roofs and hot wheels parked in the driveways. Lakewood residents are as ethnocentric as any in Dallas but they also have a very good reason to feel their area is better than all of the others, even though it is hidden away.

They have White Rock Lake, and you don't. That's a huge difference.

Until 1872 Dallas had obtained water from small springs or wells which every homeowner and business drilled on his own property. That year Browder Springs was tapped at City Park (now called Old City Park), and all the old wells became obsolete.

That was great for about 15 years, then Dallas outgrew the water supply. It seemed that 300,000 gallons a day was no longer sufficient, so in 1888 the city built a pump station in Oak Lawn, near Dallas. The new station was able to pump 10,000,000 gallons a day from the Trinity River. That station is being restored as an arts center and is visible from the Dallas North Tollway as it crosses over Harry Hines. The unique-looking structure has baffled motorists for years because nobody seemd to know what the heck it was.

The Oak Lawn pumping station was working perfectly, but by 1896 the Trinity River pollution from upstream Fort Worth was so bad a new pumping station had to be built on the Elm Fork of the Trinity at Record Crossing (near the pre-

*Old Turtle Creek pump station.*

sent intersection of Mockingbird and Stemmons Freeway).

Back in those days, remember, the Trinity River was not where it is now. The river, as a matter of fact, used to flow right to the edge of downtown, near the site of the Kennedy Assassination.

Justin F. Kimball, the former superintendent of Dallas Schools, had this to say about the Trinity in the 1920s:

"During the dry summer and fall months the sluggish current . . . is a slow-moving, black stagnant, stinking liquid, giving off great quantities of sulphurous acid gas. This gas is foul of odor, dangerous to health, and injurious to paint and other types of property. In most of the water below Fort Worth and Dallas for many miles you will find no fish or other water creatures living; they have all been poisoned by the sewage in the stream. It is dangerous to drink water from the Trinity River or from wells near it for many miles below our city. It is also at times dangerous to drink milk from cows that drink this river water."

Because of the smell, but even more because of the continued threat of flooding, a movement began to try to straighten out the river and put it between two large levees. This idea originated in the Kessler Plan of 1911, which was published three years after the devastating flood of 1908.

City leaders brought back George Kessler and asked him to update his flood control plan. His ambitious plan was to move 21 million cubic yards of earth in over three and a half years and build two levees, 30 feet high, 2,000 feet apart. The project was one-twelfth the size of the massive Panama Canal effort, but it was done, after much political jockeying. By the end of the '30s the Trinity had been contained and over $20,000,000 had been spent. But the greatest long-range benefit was the land which was reclaimed from the old Trinity riverbottoms and flood plain.

Over 10,000 acres of level land was reclaimed and developed by Leslie A. Stemmons, who had previously been on the three-man board of supervisors for the City and County of Dallas Levee Improvement District. Upon his death in 1939, his sons John and Storey Stemmons continued its development, most of which took place after World War II. Their company, Trinity Industrial District Real Estate, stil exists today at 2700 Stemmons in the Stemmons Towers.

*The massive re-routing of the Trinity River.*

Besides the Stemmons family, the man who has benefited the most is Trammell Crow, who was able to use the well-located land with freeway frontage to amass his gigantic Market Center.

Crow got his start in the real estate business by offering the world a simple new concept. He built and leased attractive-looking warehouses that

*World Trade Center in Dallas.*

were fixed up, landscaped and appealing as well as usable. He spent "a little more," but suddenly *everyone* wanted a Crow warehouse.

When he built the Dallas Trade Mart, he shocked market center people in the United States by building a huge atrium in the middle for buyers to enjoy. It seems like such a trivial idea, but nobody else had done it because nobody else wanted to give up that much rentable space.

It was a gamble, but it worked. And today Trammell Crow is the biggest real estate developer in the United States. His largest Dallas projects include the World Trade Center, the InfoMart, the Anatole Hotel and the LTV Center

*Belo Mansion on Ross Avenue.*

on Ross Avenue.

Next door to the LTV Center (don't confuse it with the LTV Tower on Elm) is the Belo Mansion, named for its builder, Colonel A.H. Belo. Built in 1890 in what was a fashionable part of Dallas, the Belo Mansion is the only house still standing on a stretch of Ross which in those days looked like Swiss Avenue today.

*Colonel and Mrs. C.C. Slaughter.*

Belo, like Colonel Slaughter, was a rare breed. But unlike Slaughter, he actually earned the title Colonel in the Civil War. It was General Robert E. Lee who promoted him to colonel after Appomattox in 1865. Belo moved to Galveston, where he soon became the business manager of the *Galveston News.* He became a partner with *News* publisher Willard Richardson, and at the age of 36 took control when Richardson died. During the 1880s he sent young G.B. Dealey to find a promising new town in which to start another newspaper. Dealey came back with the recommendation that the hamlet of Dallas be the site. Belo sent him back to crank it up. Dealey started with the most modern machinery, and in 1885 the first edition of *The Dallas Morning News* rolled off the presses. Later that year Belo moved to Dallas and worked with Dealey since *The Dallas News* had bypassed *The Galveston News* in importance.

Belo, by the way, was the first man in Texas to own a telephone, buying one from a gentleman named Alexander Graham Bell in 1876.

After his death in 1901, the Belo Mansion became just another old house but wasn't torn down because it was large enough to be converted into a funeral home, which it was until the late '60s.

Back in the early '30s two of the most notorious bank robbers in American history operated out of West Dallas. Over a two-year period they killed 12 policemen and civilians, kidnapped several people and robbed untold banks and stores. Their names were Clyde Barrow and Bonnie Parker.

They were brash, they were young, and they were finally killed. So, naturally, a movie was made about them, starring Warren Beatty and Faye Dunaway. Parts of the movie were filmed in Dallas, along what is now Upper Greenville. It was a hit called "Bonnie and Clyde."

Miss Bonnie Parker got a kick out of writing poetry while they were on the road and sending her poems to the local newspapers. Her most famous one was:

"Some day they'll go down together;
They'll bury them side by side;
To few it will be grief -
To the law a relief -
*But it's death for Bonnie and Clyde*"

Her premonition came true in a big way when, on May 23, 1934, Texas Rangers, led by Frank Hamer, ambushed Bonnie and Clyde in their stolen V-8 Ford and ended their poetry near Arcadia, Louisiana. Clyde's body had 27 bullet holes, Bonnie had 50 and the Ford took 107.

Clyde was 25 years old, and Bonnie was all of 23. On her tombstone was the inscription, "The Life She Lived Will Make This World Better Off." When the two were killed it made headlines coast to coast. When their bodies were brought back to be prepared for burial, they were brought to the Loudermilk-Sparkman Funeral Home on Ross Avenue. It was Colonel Belo's old home, which in 1977 was purchased and restored by the Dallas Bar Association.

That week, thousands of people waited in sti-
fling heat to go through the funeral home to view
the bodies as they were lying in state. The line
stretched down Ross Avenue, and ice cream ven-
dors had a field day selling cool refreshments to
the tired, hot, Bonnie and Clyde body viewers.

*Bonnie Parker's funeral in Dallas.*

The intense Texas heat could be calmed by some shade and a drink of water. Thanks to the building of White Rock Lake, water for Dallasites was available.

With the Trinity River being deemed undrinkable (something nobody would argue with even today), Dallas officials dammed up Bachman Creek in 1903, making Bachman Lake (adjacent to present-day Love Field). Eight years later they built a dam at White Rock Creek, and it became a leading recreation area for Dallasites, all 2,200 acres of it.

In 1927 Garza Dam was built, backing up 63 billion gallons of water, and ultimately creating Lake Dallas, which now, for some odd reason, is called Lake Lewisville. Several other lakes have been formed over the years to serve the water needs of an ever-growing Dallas. White Rock Lake was discontinued as the city water source in 1931, and swimming was allowed.

One hot July day in 1935 there was an official count of 3,800 swimmers in White Rock Lake. In the 1950s swimming was banned at White Rock, and that ban continues today. The Bathhouse still stands on the east side of the lake, and theater groups perform there. It's now called the Bath House Cultural Center.

Today the lake offers the best urban bicycle path in Northeast Texas, in terms of safety and setting. The 9½-mile path circles the lake and allows a cyclist the pleasure of a non-auto escape. The same goes for jogging, but the runners have inherited the cyclists on the same pathway.

At 4009 West Lawther Drive, the elegant Mount Vernon estate rules over the surrounding area. It is the home built by the "richest man in the world," H.L. Hunt. It is a replica of George Washington's home near Washington D.C., except it's bigger in scale.

*H.L. Hunt, "the world's richest man."*

Hunt's widow, Ruth Ray Hunt, has continued to live at the estate. You won't be able to see it in person, but one of the large columns in front of the house has marks on it left by H.L.'s feet. He wasn't allowed to put his feet up on the columns as he relaxed in a chair on the porch, but when his wife wasn't looking, he'd do as he pleased.

Hunt would have to be given the title of the most eccentric Dallasite since John Neely Bryan. He was at least the most interesting. He made his living as a professional gambler - he was quite good and thought he was the best poker player in the world - up until the age of 39. At that point he pulled the greatest deal in oil history when he bought out Dad Joiner just as Joiner's East Texas oil field leases hit paydirt. The *Daisy Bradford #3* had been the first well to hit oil in that field, but as was the case with many oil men of the day, Joiner had oversold interests in his leases. In a way he was hoping for a dry hole, because it appeared he could use up the investors' money, then have some left over when the well proved dry.

As land owners and investors began to lean on Joiner, H.L. Hunt, a hustler in the same league with Joiner, offered to buy him out for $1,000,000.

The only catch: Hunt had only $109 to his name.

In an incredible - but true - series of events, Hunt offered $20,000 to one of Joiner's men to allow a Hunt man to monitor late breaking events at Joiner's leases; then he offered $25,000 to H.L. Williford to help Hunt find a hiding Joiner and help Hunt make a deal with Joiner; finally, he got a friend, Pete Lake, to loan him $30,000 cash. In return, Lake would get 20 percent of Hunt's deal.

It all came to a head in the Baker Hotel (now, regretably, torn down) where the two men negotiated for several days and nights. Finally, Hunt got a call from his man in East Texas. A Deep Rock Oil Company well sample showed that a big strike was hours away.

At midnight that night, November 26, 1930, in room 1553 at the Baker Hotel, Joiner and Hunt signed a contract. Joiner sold out to Hunt for $1,335,000. Of that, $30,000 was a cash down payment and the rest would be paid out of earnings. Hunt celebrated by ordering some cheese and crackers.

It wasn't until later that Joiner found out that Hunt paid $25,000 to Williford and $20,000 to his man in East Texas.

When the Deep Rock well came in, the oil fraternity went wild. Dad Joiner had found the biggest oil field in the world. But the subheads in the newspapers astonished everyone: "Joiner sells out to Hunt for $1,500,000."

Hunt immediately went to Shreveport to borrow money against his oil in the ground. The banker kicked him out of his office because Hunt was broke. Hunt came back to Dallas and talked to Nathan Adams at the First National Bank. Adams, like Fred Florence at Republic Bank, knew how profitable the oil business could be. Hunt and Adams shook hands on a banking relationship which would last over 50 years.

That East Texas oil field was the largest oil field in the world for the next 20 years, and it was no accident that Dallas, not Tyler or Shreveport, wound up as the financial hub of the oil industry for years. Over four billion barrels of oil have come from that one field.

Hunt's field brought in over $100,000,000 in profits. In the meantime, Joiner bought a home on Preston Road, divorced his wife of 52 years, married his young secretary and died penniless in 1947.

In 1936 Lake and Hunt decided to amicably split their profits. For his original $30,000 Lake was given five producing leases (worth about $4,000,000), $1,000,000 in cash, one drilling rig and one Buick. Hunt wound up with the rest, worth about $20,000,000. Not bad for someone who started with $109.

Many stories have been written about Hunt and his families, some embellished, many true. But he *was* one the great *individuals* of his time. It's hard to understand some of the things he did - he once told **Dallas Morning News** writer Frank X. Tolbert that he had fathered 78 children. But his positive influence on the city of

Dallas, both in civic and financial circles, is probably as great as any man this town has seen, especially if you include the legacies of his children.

Some of the more visible (and diverse) holdings the Hunt family members have brought to Dallas include The Crescent, Bronco Bowl in Oak Cliff, The Mansion on Turtle Creek, *D Magazine*, World Championship Tennis, Thanksgiving Tower, Reunion Tower, and numerous philanthropic offerings to Baylor Hospital, First Baptist Church, Highland Park Presbyterian Church, and many more.

Probably more than any other family in Dallas history, the Hunts have left their mark on the city and, odds are, they will do so in the next generation.

Also leaving its mark on the city over the years has been the Jewish community. One of its more hidden gifts to Dallas is the old Edgewood Addition which, between 1912 and 1920, rivaled Highland Park in affluence. South Ervay, coming south out of downtown, had been, years before Edgewood, the very first exclusive area in Dallas. Nestled next to the City Park, "The Cedars" was an inspirational collection of Victorian mansions. Today they are the site of the R.L. Thornton Freeway.

Since 90 percent of the Jewish population in Dallas lived in South Dallas at the time, they built an affluent neighborhood along Forest Avenue, now called Martin Luther King Boulevard. As the

*Mansion on South Boulevard.*

1950s approached, a national phenomenon took place in Dallas, where minorities grew in to the inner cities and middle-class whites moved to the suburbs. Such was the case with the Forest Avenue Jewish neighborhood, which moved to North Dallas to a new area north of the new Temple Emanu-El at Northwest Highway and Hillcrest.

Their old neighborhood was cut in half by the building of Central Expressway. While the west side of the area became subject to urban decay, the east side has shown a different face. The area is now predominately black.

While only one of the magnificent mansions on the west side remains today, it is no longer a residence. It is McGowan's Funeral Home at 2830 S. Ervay.

On the east side of Central Expressway, concerned leaders in the black community have banded together to preserve the beauty of the neighborhood and have been successful in receiving Dallas' second historical district designation for South Boulevard and Park Row, between Oakland and Central Expressway.

The large Prairie, Bungalow and Craftsman bungalow homes on South Boulevard feature large sleeping porches over porte-cocheres and gabled dormers. Two of the finest homes in this district were built in 1913 by J. Edward Overbeck: the Levi Marcus home at 2707 South Boulevard and the Isaac Bromberg home at 2617 South Boulevard.

Forest Avenue High School - now called James Madison - was built in 1917 and was the finest school in Dallas. Its most prominent alum is Stanley Marcus, the world famous Neiman-Marcus retailer. But Forest Lane lost the various zoning battles and was developed commercially, just like Ross Avenue.

There are hundreds of fascinating hidden places to see in Dallas, but the South Boulevard/ Park Row Historical District is, without doubt, the most hidden. Out of over 1,000,000 people in Dallas, probably 99.9 percent have never seen

*Stanley Marcus and daughter.*

*South Boulevard/Park Row Historical District.*

it. But thanks to several affluent black professionals, the area thrives and is available for the rest of Dallas to see. Thanks to them, this area is not merely a memory, like the rest of the magnificent Forest Lane neighborhood.

Right down the street is Fair Park, one of the feathers in Dallas' cap. It was the persistence and expert salesmanship of R.L. Thornton, Sr. that allowed Dallas to win the bid for the 1936 Texas Centennial, over Houston, San Antonio and Austin. Dallas offered $10,000,000 in cash and property, the State Fair site, the addition of a fine arts museum, a natural history museum, a horticulture building, an aquarium and an amphitheater. In all, over 50 buildings were devoted to the Centennial, including the dramatic Hall of State, which was (and is) fronted by the 1,000-foot long esplanade and reflecting pool, lined by art deco-style exhibition buildings.

Gone are the popular burlesque "strip" shows at Fair Park, but the area is still chock-full of museums and other points of interest which were updated for the Texas Sesquicentennial Celebration in 1986.

*Texas Centennial celebration in 1936.*

The Cotton Bowl (1930) is still there, although "the house that Doak Walker built" hosts only two major football games per year now - the Cotton Bowl Classic and the Texas-Oklahoma game. Although its glory days were indeed the Doak Walker days, the Cotton Bowl is the only stadium in the world which has been the home stadium for three NFL teams which have won Super Bowl Championships. The Dallas Cowboys (obviously), the Dallas Texans (which went on to become the Kansas City Chiefs) and the 1952 Dallas Texans (which later became the Baltimore Colts, now in Indianapolis).

Speaking of Super Bowl, few people realize that Dallas' Lamar Hunt was the man most instrumental in creating the nation's most popular single sporting event. In August of 1959, 27-year-old Lamar Hunt co-chaired a meeting of the owners of the new American Football Association. They formed the AFL to compete with the gigantic NFL, and it was a tough battle. Hunt was losing up to $1,000,000 per year, which spawned one of the great quotes in the history of Dallas. "At this rate," one writer remarked, "Lamar Hunt will go broke in 100 years."

In 1963 Hunt signed a $36 million television contract with NBC, and the AFL, with Hunt as its president, was here to stay. Later, in April of 1966, while running to catch a plane at Love Field, Hunt ran into Dallas Cowboy General Manager Tex Schramm. The two started talking

114

*Another sell-out crowd at the Cotton Bowl.*

football under the statue of the Texas Ranger, and Hunt decided to catch a later flight to Houston. The two walked out to Hunt's car and sat there for an hour and a half, discussing a merger between the NFL and AFL. It was an historic conversation for professional football because after more formal negotiations ensued, the two leagues merged two months later. On June 8, 1966, Hunt, Schramm and NFL Commissioner Pete Rozelle announced in New York that the NFL and AFL would unite.

And few people realize that it was Lamar Hunt's daughter, Sharron, who was responsible for coming up with the name "Super Bowl." She was out in the driveway of the Hunt estate in North Dallas playing with her "super ball" when her dad was trying to come up with a shorter name for the AFC-NFC World Professional Football Championship Game. Hunt talked to his daughter about it and came up with the name.

So in a backyard in North Dallas, the Super Bowl was born.

And the rest has become history.

*Las Colinas, "the first city of the 21st century.*

# LAS COLINAS

If you have a fascination with the City of Dallas as it stands today, you can learn much about it by studying and understanding its past. But to see its future one must find an example of Dallas' tomorrow, today.

Such is the case at Las Colinas.

Located in North Irving, between Dallas and D/FW International Airport, Las Colinas is one of the world's most highly acclaimed real estate developments. International urban planners refer to Las Colinas as "the first city of the 21st century."

Surprisingly few Dallasites have actually taken the time to slip off the John W. Carpenter Freeway and see Las Colinas firsthand. Not only is there nothing like it in Dallas, there is nothing like it in the world. The polar opposite of the 100-year-old pioneer buildings of Hidden Dallas, this venture, tucked away in one of the Dallas bedroom communities, represents the "highest and best use" of well-located, valuable raw land. And it represents the spirit of Dallas, which grew and matured into a major international center because of the drive, energy, and vision of its individual leaders - in this case, the Carpenter family.

Seeing the giant cranes dot the sky at Las Colinas is the tangible evidence of Ben Carpenter's vision, as progress forces him to develop his beloved ranchland.

And his vision is so far-sighted, and his efforts for a first-class city so strong, that one can look at Las Colinas today and actually see the Dallas of tomorrow.

Las Colinas is a 12,000-acre master-planned development, devoting a full 4,000 acres to greenbelts, parklands, countryside and walkways. The last time a man in this region took that much space and put it back as "public land" was when John Armstrong conceived Highland Park back in 1906.

The area, for years, was the Carpenter family ranch, known as Hackberry Creek Ranch. Mrs. John W. Carpenter refered to it as "El Ranchito de Las Colinas," or "the little ranch of the hills."

John W. Carpenter (1881-1959) was a self-made man who started in his native Corsicana checking power lines along lonely stretches of Texas highways. During his career he became

*Mandalay Canal.*

one of the most influential Texans ever. As president of Texas Power and Light (for 22 years) he was credited with bringing electricity to West Texas. He was a leader in the founding of Texas Tech University, he founded Lone Star Steel and he started the Texas Security Life Insurance Company, which ultimately became Southland Life Insurance Company.

He was the developer of the Southland Center, Dallas' first *true* modern skyscraper. When it was dedicated in the late '50s it was the tallest building west of the Mississippi River, and it ushered in a new era for downtown Dallas. It was the seventh largest privately-owned building complex in the world at the time.

Meanwhile, back at the ranch, the small town of Irving crept along like hundreds of other sleepy towns in Texas. The Hackberry Creek Ranch was being turned over to the next generation as Ben Carpenter and his wife, Betty, raised their children on the ranch and at their townhome in Highland Park. In 1973, when the Dallas/Fort Worth Airport was built just west of the ranch, Ben Carpenter and his brother-in-law, Dan C. Williams, were already taking steps to do the inevitable - develop the ranch. Encroaching development, higher taxes and skyrocketing land values forced them to move the cattle off to other ranches and hire a legion of architects, landscape specialists, urban planners and real estate specialists. They then donated much of the right-of-way for a freeway connecting the north side of the new airport with Dallas.

What Carpenter envisioned was not based on other developments he'd seen. Las Colinas would be something which had not existed before. It would be a master-planned, mixed-use development with skyscrapers, mansions, hotels, canals, parks, creeks, apartments, shopping centers, condominiums, neighborhoods, warehouse districts, schools, churches, lakes, restaurants, golf courses, movie studios, equestrian areas, and a spirit of community among the 100,000 people who would live or work there.

Ben Carpenter envisioned *excellence* in every facet of the development. He gave up certain short term profits in order to build out a first-class dream which would take over 20 years. He wanted something which *future* generations of residents could enjoy. And by sticking to his dream, he has built a city within a city which is the prototype of urban planning going into the 21st century.

While the land was still a prairie, the first thing he did was build the 125-acre Lake Carolyn (named for his sister, Carolyn Williams) and through a series of canals, connected the present and future buildings of the Urban Center. Now water taxis and a water bus make regular trips from the Mandalay Canal to other stops at the Dallas Marriott Hotel, the magnificent Williams Square complex and other buildings on the lake

121

*Laying tracks for the Area Personal Transit.*

and canal. Although it's a novelty today, in the future it wil be a key transportation source.

Another unique Las Colinas mode of transportation is the soon-to-be-completed APT (Area Personal Transit), a $32 million above-the-ground transportation system in the Urban center (downtown area of Las Colinas). When complete in the summer of 1989, the ATP will consist of eight miles of track and connect 1,000 acres of the Urban Center.

Each vehicle will be computer driven - similar to the AirTrans system at the Dallas/Fort Worth International Airport - and will seat 12-16 people, accommodating about 70 people per trip. Each car will be air conditioned. The Dallas County Utility and Reclamation district, in conjunction with Westinghouse Electric Corporation, designed the elevated trains. Westinghouse manufactured similar systems for Tampa, Miami, Las Vegas, Orlando, Atlanta and London Gatwick airports.

While waiting for the APT to be completed, Las Colinas residents and visitors have already taken to the water for their futuristic transportation. The Las Colinas Water Taxis - mahogany motorboats (with indoor cabins) which were brought over from Venice, Italy - run nonstop during the day along the Mandalay Canal, the

*Water Bus at Las Colinas.*

*Mandalay Canal at Las Colinas.*

man-made waterway linking the buildings of the Urban Center via Lake Carolyn's water supply. Stops along the way include excellent shops and boutiques as well as fine restaurants. The best place to catch the water taxi is in front of the Catarina Cafe, one of the best places in Dallas/Fort Worth for Mexican food al fresco.

The Catarina Cafe is located at the base of the medieval clock tower, which is visible from the John W. Carpenter Freeway. The Mandalay Canal was designed to be invisible from the roads and highways, and it is.

In one of the smartest design moves you'll find in the area, the Old English storefronts on the west side of the Mandalay Canal are actually false fronts. Behind them is a multi-story parking garage. Never before has a parking garage had such a pleasant visual quality.

*Passenger pick-up for Water Bus.*

*Sculptor Robert Glen and his Mustangs at Las Colinas.*

Cafe Cipriani and Eric's Texas Cafe are two other recommended places to dine along the canal. There is Hip Pocket Sandwich Shop and a Wendy's for those who prefer a quicker, less expensive meal.

The best time to visit the Mandalay Canal is during CanalFest, held each spring and fall. Dancers, musicians, clowns and other family entertainment help make CanalFest a fun-filled event each year.

Around the corner from the Mandalay Canal is the Williams Square office complex, on O'Connor Boulevard. The three-building complex overlooks one of the most breathtaking works of art in the world - The Mustangs of Las Colinas.

Nine bronze larger-than-life mustangs are frozen in mid-stride as they gallop across the Williams Square Plaza through a cascading stream. The one-and-a-half-times-life-size sculptures were created with marvelous detail by world-famous wildlife artist Robert Glen of Nairobi, Kenya. Commissioned by Ben Carpenter, Glen took seven years of painstaking work to create what is the largest equestrian sculpture in the world.

Carpenter wanted to make a statement with the sculpture. His vision and Glen's skills brought about a work of art which captures the spirit and heritage of Texas and the southwest. It has quickly become a symbol of Las Colinas and its "superior class" point of view.

The Mustangs of Las Colinas are simply astonishing. Seeing them in person is one of the requisites of living in or visiting Dallas. When picking up someone from D/FW Airport, come back to Dallas on Carpenter Freeway (the north route on Highway 114) and take a quick exit on O'Connor. Williams Square is located two blocks east of Carpenter Freeway on O'Connor Boulevard. It's the perfect introduction to Dallas.

If you want to make a meal out of it, the adjacent Mustang Cafe has some of the best southwestern cuisine in the region. Try the jalapeno cornbread and the pecan-fried chicken. It's a culinary religious experience. And the entire east wall is a glass panoramic view of the Mustangs, the best view in the southwest for enjoying "home cooking." You might take note that between the bar and the restaurant are two small sculptures of mustangs. They were created by Robert Glen and are on loan to the Mustang Cafe by Ben Carpenter.

The concierge at Williams Square can help you call up a water taxi, which can meet you and your party at a taxi dock behind Williams Square for a ride to the Marriott Mandalay Dallas Hotel at Las Colinas or to the Catarina Cafe stop on the Mandalay Canal. Rides are 50¢ each way. Again, this is a Dallas necessity.

Las Colinas is perceived by many Dallasites as strictly a business center. Indeed, it is the national or regional headquarters for over 750 major corporations. And the Urban Center, when built out, will be larger than downtown Dallas. Companies such as Xerox, The Associates, Caltex, Zale's, IBM, Boy Scouts of America, Fidelity Investments, and Ranch Publishing call Las Colinas home.

Although over 50,000 people work in Las Colinas, over 20,000 now live there. The median income of the average Las Colinas homeowner is the same as the average Highland Park resident. And in early 1987, the average cost of a new home in Las Colinas was the same as the average Park Cities home. The exclusive Fox Glen, Cottonwood Valley and Country Club Place residential neighborhoods all have 24-hour security at the front gates, so seeing them in person is difficult, unless prior permission is obtained. But the University Hills residential neighborhood is not restricted and is one of the most inspiring new developments in the North Texas area. The homes are magnificent, and the rolling hills ("las colinas") provide a Dallas natural beauty rivaled only by Oak Cliff's wonderful Kessler Park. University Hills is located west of Carpenter Freeway between Rochelle and Wingren.

Another Hidden Dallas feature found in Las Colinas is the Lakeshore Apartments, located next to the Marriott Mandalay Dallas Hotel on Lake Carolyn. A mid-rise apartment complex, Lakeshore overlooks the lake. Residents are able to take a water taxi to work each day in the Urban Center. Apartment living in the Dallas area will be redefined by Lakeshore Apartments.

As the 1990s approach, Las Colinas - which was a working cattle ranch in 1975 - now boasts over 150 retail shops, dozens of restaurants and over 30 financial institutions serving the area. The long-awaited Irvine Ranch Farmers Market brings another unique Dallas "first," while the Las Colinas Sports Club remains one of America's state-of-the-art sports complexes. The site of the Byron Nelson Classic, the Sports Club has 36 championship holes, including a first hole green shaped like the state of Texas, with a sand trap shaped like Oklahoma and a water hazard in the shape of the Gulf of Mexico. The course is available to guests of the adjacent Four Seasons Inn and Conference Center - again, a state-of-the-art facility.

*Golf remains popular in Dallas.*

Besides the two 18-hole courses at the Las Colinas Sports Club, there are three more courses in the area: The Las Colinas Country Club, Hackberry Creek Country Club and the L.B. Houston municipal golf course. The Las Colinas Country Club hosts the annual Marilyn Smith Founders' Classic, the frontrunner to the Ladies Professional Golf Association's Senior Tournament.

The Las Colinas Equestrian Center is the finest facility of its kind in the southwest. Located at Royal Lane and O'Connor, this exquisite Spanish-style complex, with a two-tiered terra cotta roof, is home to over 100 horses. The center also hosts the annual Las Colinas Grand Prix, one of the top three equestrian events in America each year.

Across O'Connor from the Equestrian Center is the Dallas Communications Complex and its nucleus, the Studios at Las Colinas. Developed by Trammell S. Crow, this 100-acre complex features motion picture production studios and over 100 production, video, music and production-related companies. It is quite a stimulating work environment for feature and industrial film and video production staff members, who congregate at the complex's Studio C Restaurant - which is open to the public.

The big misconception in Dallas is that The Studios at Las Colinas are another Hollywood. Several major motion pictures ("Silkwood,"

*The Dallas Communications Complex.*

"Streamers," "Robo Cop" and more) have been filmed there, but The Studios at Las Colinas does not produce any movies. It rents the proper facilities, such as sound stages, dressing rooms, etc. to producers. The largest percentage of the business produced at the Studios is the industrial, or commercial, type of production. It's a very big business in Dallas in general - at the Studios, specifically.

In recent years, the Studios, with the $10 million soundstages, have enjoyed the reputation of having the best, most technically sophisticated production facility in the world. Many Los Angeles and New York music video producers and concert promoters have used the Studios to film elaborate music videos and rehearse for national tours. Many of the most prominent names in the music business have used the Studios at Las Colinas to work out the elaborate sound, lighting and special effects used in most of today's concert productions.

One staff member recalls Julian Lennon's bus pulling up to the Studios, and seeing Lennon hop out, skateboard in hand, and head for Royal Lane for some serious skateboard riding. Lennon's crew quickly caught him and pointed him back to the studio.

Although many tourists looking for a Universal Studio-type tour are disappointed in the complex, it is an interesting place to look around. The outdoor mall features a huge mural on the west wall. One unknown fact is that the mural has a family pictured in it for no apparent reason. Actually, it is the artist and his family. He used a self-portrait as a means of signing his work.

On the far southeast corner of Las Colinas is a futuristic-looking building with several large satellite dishes. This is the Dallas/Fort Worth Teleport, one of the largest of its kind in the country. Companies in Las Colinas and Dallas/Fort Worth can send or receive video signals from satellites 24,000 miles up in the sky. The entire world is a split-second away via teleport transmission.

Many of the national and international events you see on your television were "downlinked" to your home via the D/FW Teleport. Again, it is among the finest, most up-to-date teleports in America today.

While the newness of Las Colinas is dazzling to both the local tourist and the international urban planner, the area does have two specific timeless geographical points of interest, which can be seen today. One is California Crossing, located off of Rochelle, between Northwest Highway (Spur 348) and the Carpenter Freeway. A street, still called California Crossing, runs into Rochelle just after it crosses over the Trinity River on the east side of Las Colinas. That site is the second most historic Trinity River crossing in the Dallas area. The first, of course, is the site John Neely Bryan chose as the Trinity River crossing where he started the town of Dallas. California Crossing was the popular spot to cross the river during the early 1850s, when hundreds of gold prospectors headed to California for the gold rush.

As they reached the mesquite-covered rolling hills west of the Trinity, now called Las Colinas, they encountered herds of wild mustangs roaming the land, free and undomesticated. The spirit of that freedom and adventure is captured in the bronze Mustangs of Las Colinas, located where the horses ran free 100 years before on that very spot.

To the west of California Crossing is Turkey

*Stars and Stripes overlook Las Colinas countryside.*

*Parking garage door on the Mandalay Canal*

Knob, now the site of the University of Dallas. It is one of the highest points in Dallas County and was, for years, the lookout point for the Indians who lived in the area.

While seeing the interesting hidden spots in Las Colinas, you might stop at Texas Stadium, which is not so hidden. The pride of Irving, Texas Stadium is the home of the Dallas Cowboys. (The football club itself now headquarters in Valley Ranch, a section of Irving north of Las Colinas.) Tours of Texas Stadium are available, and soon the Dallas Cowboys Center in Valley Ranch will have a complex set up for Cowboys fans, which will feature everything you ever wanted to see or know about America's Team.

The 7-Eleven in Valley Ranch is known as the Cowboy 7-Eleven. Most of the players and coaches stop there before and after work. Several players live in Valley Ranch, so seeing Cowboys is an everyday part of life in that neighborhood.

And the neighborhoods continue to grow despite a down real estate market.

In the second half of 1986, Las Colinas made up over 70 percent of the luxury townhome sales in the entire Dallas region. There are exciting things happening in Las Colinas, and the vision which Ben Carpenter has nurtured over the years is now a reality.

Not everybody can go out and start a city from scratch. And Las Colinas, a mixed-use, master-planned development which is part of the City of Irving, is the culmination of one man's vision and the "superior quality" element of that vision.

Ben Carpenter turned the controls of the

*Las Colinas.*

*Mandalay Canal.*

Southland Financial Corporation over to his son, John W. Carpenter III, in early 1987. Dallas and Texas were experiencing the worst real estate recession since the Great Depression. But the Carpenter family has fought to keep control of the empire they have guided for three generations.

The small touches, such as the pleasant stonework on all the overpasses on the Carpenter Freeway as it passes through Las Colinas, are the ideas of Ben Carpenter. There are no ugly, square glass buildings in Las Colinas because, well, because he didn't like the look of them. He wanted the buildings and the necessary parking garages to blend in with the environment. And he loves flowers. As a matter of fact, when he couldn't find a nursery to supply Las Colinas with the flowers he desired, he started his own nursery and landscaping service at Las Colinas. About 400,000 flowers are planted every year by that company.

Las Colinas was designed to be a long-lasting, total living and working environment. Under the Carpenters' careful scrutiny and demand for excellence, Las Colinas has become just that. It's one of the most impressive developments in America today and is something Dallasites should see firsthand.

The Las Colinas of today is the Dallas of tomorrow.

*Sanger Brothers' first airmail delivery.*

# FIRSTS

Dallasites, like most Texans, spend plenty of time dwelling on how their city is the biggest, best, first or most important in various categories. Everybody should have a certain amount of ammo when it comes to bragging rights, and Dallas residents are blessed with a healthy proportion.

As the years have gone on, most Dallasites pointed to America's Team (The Dallas Cowboys) as the most impressive image in the eyes of the rest of America, at least when the Cowboys were in the midst of a record-breaking streak of winning seasons. To many locals, Roger Staubach should be either ordained or crowned at any given moment, because his legend continues to endure and grow, more than any other Dallasite in modern history.

Dallas is the home of many firsts. All cities have firsts, but most cities on both coasts were founded at least 200 years before Big D and have a head start. But when it comes to business

- ranging from airlines to retail - Dallas has been the first in several national and international endeavors.

American Airlines and United Airlines have roots in Dallas, while Braniff, Southwest and TranStar (RIP) all have headquartered in Big D.

The center for aviation in Dallas, up until the largest airport in the world was built between Dallas and Fort Worth, was Love Field.

Built in 1917 as a training center for the Army's air training, Love Field was named for Lt. Moss Lee Love, a young Army flier who was killed in a plane crash in California. Ten years after it was built, the City of Dallas bought it and made it one of the first municipal airports in the country. Up until the '50s its terminals were located on Lemmon Avenue.

Just after World War I, aviation in America entered its heyday, and public interest was stirred by many record-breaking flights made all over the globe by pioneer pilots of the day. Few people realize that several of these world-famous flights had Dallas connections.

On August 19, 1927, Dallasite "Lone Star Bill" Erwin took off in the *Dallas Spirit* from Oakland, Calif., and headed west in an attempt to be the first man to fly across the Pacific Ocean - from California to Hong Kong.

He was also planning to continue west and make an around-the-world flight in record time. The first leg was Dallas to San Francisco, and the

*Braniff DC-6 and American DC-3 at Love Field.*

next leg was the Bay area to Honolulu - part of the famed Dole Air Race. He was to continue on to Hong Kong and collect a $25,000 prize offered to anyone in the world who would be the first to fly across the Pacific. The prize was offered by a wealthy Dallas aviation enthusiast named Colonel Bill Easterwood.

The day after Easterwood announced the prize, Erwin announced he would accept the challenge.

143

Erwin, a World War I ace pilot, was a Top Gun of his era. Credited with downing eight enemy aircraft, Erwin was called the most valuable American aviator of the war by Colonel Billy Mitchell. Erwin had won both the Distinguished Service Cross and the French Croix de Guerre.

"Lone Star Bill" didn't have the money for an airplane which could make the trip, so *The Dallas Morning News* led the fund raising for a new plane. *Dallas Spirit* was, of course, a name inspired by Charles Lindbergh's *Spirit of St. Louis,* which was the hottest item in the world after successfully navigating the Atlantic ocean by air for the first time.

Easterwood, a Dallas capitalist, aviator, philanthropist and unofficial goodwill ambassador, had offered to pay Lindbergh's taxes on the $25,000 he won for his flight across the Atlantic. He then offered prizes of $25,000 each for the first person to fly from Dallas to Paris, from Dallas to Rome and from Dallas to Hong Kong.

Erwin, caught up in the hoopla of the Lindbergh success, took off from Oakland, Calif., on August 19, 1927. His young wife was not permitted to go because she was under 21, so a wireless operator accompanied "Lone Star Bill" on his record flight.

A little over 200 miles from San Francisco, the operator radioed back that the *Dallas Spirit* had just recovered from a tailspin. Moments later, the plane disappeared and was never seen or heard from again.

One can only guess the ramifications of Erwin's feat, had it been successful. But unlike Lindbergh, who enjoyed worldwide acclaim the rest of his life, "Lone Star Bill" and his *Dallas Spirit* died amidst his bold dreams.

Six weeks later, when just about all hope of finding the *Dallas Spirit* was gone, none other than Charles A. Lindbergh, flying his ultra-famous *Spirit of St. Louis,* swooped into town to dedicate the Dallas Municipal Airport, Love Field. A crowd of 10,000 waited for him there.

*Dallas Air Carnival at Love Field.*

What was described as the largest gathering in Dallas to date - 100,000 people - lined the parade route along Preston Road and on into downtown as America's idol was driven to the Adolphus Hotel. That night at the hotel, over 700 Dallasites paid tribute to the Lone Eagle.

Three years later two Frenchmen, Maurice Belmonte and Dieudonne Coste, accepted Col. Easterwood's challenge to fly from Paris to Dallas. After only one stop in New York for refueling, the duo flew into Love Field, where a whopping 25,000 shouting Dallasites cheered them in. It was the first trans-Atlantic flight from east to west, in September of 1930.

Col. Easterwood gladly paid the French aviators their $25,000, but he never paid the Dallas-Hong Kong or Dallas-Rome prizes. There were no successful flights for those two.

Easterwood died in 1940, but he declared shortly before his death, "What America needs is 50,000 planes and 100,000 pilots."

Another Dallasite, Morris M. Titterington, is credited with some of the most important discoveries in the field of aviation. He perfected a stabilizer to prevent planes from turning over in the air, and he also invented the earth induction compass that made possible Charles Lindbergh's trans-Atlantic flight. He was killed in a plane crash in Pennsylvania in 1928.

Another incident, before the turn of the century, could have made Dallas one of the nation's sports hotbeds, but it was nixed by the governor of Texas.

A Dallas promoter and saloonkeeper named Dan Stuart gave a check for $41,000 to the proper boxing officials as an earnest money payment to bring to Dallas the greatest heavyweight boxing championship ever held. It was a fight between "Gentleman" Jim Corbett and "Fighting Bob" Fitzsimmons.

Construction began in the summer of 1895 on a giant, wooden, octagonal stadium which would hold 53,000 spectators for the fight.

Railroads advertised widely that they would run excursions from all parts of the country for the fight - but protests from all over the city and state caused Governor Charles Culberson to call a special session of the Texas Legislature to pass an ironclad law to prevent this "affront to the moral sense and progress of Texas."

Only weeks before the big fight was scheduled to be held in Dallas, the law banning prize fighting in Texas passed, forcing the fight to be moved to New Orleans.

Watching all this with keen interest was Judge Roy Bean of Langtry, the "Law West of the Pecos." One of Texas' great promoters himself, he contacted Fitzsimmons and the Irish boxing champion, Peter Maher, and arranged for what Judge Bean called a "world championship fight." Of course, the Texas Legislature had just passed the law banning prize fighting, so when the Texas

Rangers came riding in to stop the fight, the good judge showed them where the fight was going to be held - on a sandbar in the Rio Grande, which Judge Bean ruled was in Mexico. The Rangers had no jurisdiction in Mexico, so they left.

Five train-loads of boxing fans made the 380-mile trip from El Paso to Langtry for the fight on February 21, 1896. Other trains came from the East. The sandbar was between two canyon walls and this made for a natural amphitheater. Judge Bean charged $20 per person and sold a large quantity of cold beer at $1 a bottle.

When newspaper reporters told the Judge that his fight was not really a recognized world championship bout, he said "This fight is *too* for the world's championship. And *that's* my ruling!"

The Texas Rangers had summoned assistance from Mexican authorities, and they dispatched some rurales to stop the fight, but they arrived too late. The fight lasted less than a minute. Fitzsimmons caught Maher with a nasty right to the jaw and the fight was over as soon as it began.

One of the New York sportswriters covering the fight was former gunslinger Bat Masterson. His story on the fight in Langtry began with, "That Fitz is the fastest creature alive."

One of the great sporting traditions in Dallas these days is the ever-popular Texas-Oklahoma football game, played every October at the Cotton Bowl during the State Fair of Texas.

A little known forerunner of this game was the

annual Texas Heavyweights vs. the Sooner State Eleven in the early 1900s. It was held during the fair and was quite a popular exhibition football game, although neither team represented a school. The Heavyweights team was the first organized football team in Dallas, which had no affiliation. A railway provided their uniforms. Some of the players included were Hugh Prather, Roy Munger, Jimmy Adams and John Frick.

The first University of Texas - University of Oklahoma football game in Dallas took place on October 19, 1918. At the time, OU was a member of the Southwest Conference.

The Southwest Athletic Conference was formed in Dallas on May 6, 1914, when representatives of seven schools met to create a league for some of the larger schools in the southwest. They met at the Oriental Hotel, later the site of the Baker Hotel, and now the site of the Southwestern Bell building. The athletic director of the University of Texas extended the invitations to representatives from Baylor, Southwestern, Oklahoma A&M, Texas A&M, Louisiana State, Arkansas and Texas.

They completed the organization on December 8 of that year at a meeting at the Rice Hotel in Houston. Representatives of Rice and Oklahoma were present for that meeting and joined the others (LSU had dropped out) to be charter members of the SWC. Southwestern, Oklahoma, Phillips, and Oklahoma A&M (later Oklahoma

State) ultimately withdrew from the conference while Southern Methodist and Texas Christian were added.

Then in 1956 Texas Tech joined, and in 1971 the University of Houston was added.

The SWC office remains in Dallas, and the Cotton Bowl Classic is still closely tied to the conference.

The annual Texas-OU game, as we know it, was initiated in 1929. For years prior to that, the Texas Longhorns played Vanderbilt for the State Fair exhibition game.

There have been other firsts, which are tangible, even today. The Steak and Ale restaurant on Lemmon Avenue is the first Steak and Ale ever built, and it continues to be the flagship location for a nationwide network of restaurants.

The originator of the concept is Dallasite Norman Brinker, who came to this area from San Diego. He had been a member of the U.S. Olympic Equestrian team and married Maureen Connolly, the internationally famous tennis star of the 1950s. Brinker was working with a man who was developing the concept of drive-thru windows for fast food eateries. The man had less than a dozen Jack-in-the-Box restaurants when he asked Brinker if he wanted to take charge of the southwest expansion of this new concept. Brinker jumped at the chance, and moved his wife and two small daughters to Dallas.

While business was booming for Brinker, he

lost his wife, "Little Mo," to cancer. A movie, "Little Mo," has been made about the popular former Wimbledon champion. Their daughter, Cindy Brinker, launched what has become one of the largest cancer fundraisers in the country, "A Weekend to Wipe Out Cancer," at Norman Brinker's Willow Bend Polo and Hunt Club.

Brinker sold his interest in Steak and Ale to Pillsbury, making him the largest individual stockholder of the giant corporation. He later accepted the presidency of Pillsbury's Burger King division.

A few years ago Brinker - the entrepreneur - left Burger King and bought a young Dallas growth company called Chili's.

Cashing out of Chili's was its creator, Larry Lavine. A Highland Park native, Lavine owned and operated one of North Dallas' top teenage dance clubs of all time - The Studio Club in Preston Center, which had its heyday in the early '60s.

He then opened a restaurant at the corner of Lovers Lane and Greenville, calling it Kitty Hawk. The concept was good, but not great. (The interior featured a real airplane in the middle of the room.)

Always wanting to enter the burger market, he opened the first Chili's at the corner of Greenville and Meadow. That concept appeared to offer more promise, so when the decision came to expand Kitty Hawk or Chili's, he went with Chili's.

The concept has spawned many imitators but

*Old Southland Ice House.*

grew to a healthy size before Brinker bought out Lavine, making him a multi-millionaire.

Of all the Dallas firsts (at least the ones known outside of Dallas), the most fascinating took place back in 1927, at the corner of 12th and Edgefield in the Oak Cliff section of Dallas.

John Jefferson Green, 55, was known throughout Oak Cliff as Uncle Johnny. He was the manager of an ice house, which three months before had been purchased by a new company called Southland Ice.

Ice, in the days before refrigeration, was an important quantity in the preservation of food and the ever-important chilling of beer. Hundreds of ice delivery carts roamed the streets of Dallas during the non-winter days, supplying ice blocks for home iceboxes, the forerunners of today's refrigerators.

At Uncle Johnny's ice dock, where people came by to pick up their day's supply of ice, they were surprised to find Uncle Johnny selling bread, eggs and milk along with the ice.

Well, heck, they dropped by everyday anyway. It would save them a trip to the market, so they bought bread, eggs and milk from Uncle Johnny.

Knowing he had a good idea, he went to a 26-year-old executive of Southland Ice he had met - Joe C. Thompson, Jr.

Thompson had impressed Uncle Johnny as a sharp, innovative businessman who was going

*Early 7-Elevens.*

places in the ice business. So Green, who was twice the age of his superior, Thompson, approached him with an innovative marketing proposal. If Thompson (or the company, actually) would front him the money, he would stock his particular ice house with 12 items (bread, eggs, milk, cigarettes, etc.) and sell them over the winter months when the ice business was off.

The next spring, Uncle Johnny waltzed into Thompson's office and handed him $1,000 in cash - his share of Uncle Johnny's profits.

It was at that moment that the "convenience store" concept was born.

Young Jodie Thompson eventually took control of Southland Ice and did wonders with it. The company today is one of the largest retailers in the world - The Southland Corporation, which employs 70,000 people worldwide and boasts revenues (1986) of over $12 billion (mostly through its 7-Eleven division), is the sixth largest retailer in America.

Originally, when Southland Ice turned its ice docks into "convenience stores," someone came up with the grand idea to use a totem pole as a symbol for this new concept, because people "toted" away their purchases. It was approved and the stores became known as Tote'm Stores.

One day a confused group of Indians in Alaska received an order for several large handmade totem poles, and soon all the convenience stores in the world - all two dozen of them - had one out front.

In 1931, when Jody Thompson was named president of Southland Ice, another prominent leadership role awaited him. On March 31 he took over Southland Ice and one week later, on April 7, he was elected to Dallas' first city council. The city had just adopted the city council-city manager form of government that year.

And that year Jody Thompson turned 30 years old.

His company continued to flourish, but only in Oak Cliff. It wasn't until he had over 60 locations, mostly in Fort Worth and Oak Cliff, that he ventured north of the Trinity River, purchasing City Ice in 1943. They had already started their own dairy in Oak Cliff (called Oak Farms Dairy), and the age of the modern convenience store began on January 24, 1946, when the board of directors of the company changed the Tote'm name to a new name the stores use today.

The Tracy-Locke advertising agency was hired to come up with a new name and identity for the convenience store chain. It was suggested by Tracy-Locke that all the stores remain open from 7 a.m. to 11 p.m. and be called 7-Eleven Stores.

And the rest - 9,000 stores later - is history.

Jody Thompson's son's, John, Jere, and Joe, Jr., began to take Southland private in 1987, in the second largest takeover transaction in American business history - worth over $5 billion.

*The Wine Press was called J. Alfred's.*

That'a a lot of bread, milk and eggs.

Somewhere in that big convenience store in the sky, Joe C. Thompson must surely be smiling, knowing that in 1988, his dream of the Thompsons owning all of the Southland Corportation stock was close to becoming a reality.

When you stop at the 7-Eleven on 12th and Edgefield, think of Joe C. Thompson, think of the magnitude of the Southland empire. Then remember that it was Uncle Johnny Green and his little concept that went from that small Oak Cliff corner to every corner of the world - including Japan, where there are currently over 1,000 7-Elevens.

Another sacred spot in Dallas is on Oak Lawn, just south of Herschel, where a small restaurant called the Wine Press can be found. About 15 years ago, two men struck up a conversation at a bar and decided that they could make money in the bar-restaurant business. They put together some capital, and Gene Street and Phil Cobb started a little place called J. Alfred's, from the T.S. Eliot poem about J. Alfred Prufrock. The name of their corporation, which outlived their first bar, was Prufrock.

The two new restaurateurs served free nuts in their beer joint, and soon J. Alfred's was a favorite hangout for motorcycle gangs looking for some cold beer. Those were wild days for the front man, Street, and the behind-the-scenes man, Cobb. Regardless of what you might want

161

to say about J. Alfred's, it made money. Street and Cobb expanded, experimenting with various concepts and styles, before deciding on two similar restaurant themes, Dixie House and Black-Eyed Pea, both serving home-cooked meals and a warm price.

Both the Black-Eyed Pea and the Dixie House names went over everywhere, and in 1986 Street and Cobb sold their interest in Prufrock for $45 million. Street took his money and moved to Hawaii, while Cobb remains in Dallas, investing in several properties and businesses, including *The Dallas Downtown News.* The two still own SRO, a nightclub on McKinney (across from their first Dixie House) and the Wine Press, located on Oak Lawn where their first bar - J. Alfred's - got them started.

Street once accepted a bet to not cut his hair for a year, won the bet and to date still keeps his hair at shoulder length.

It's hard to drive through Dallas and not find a Dixie House or Black-Eyed Pea, but it's harder to drive through and not see a McDonald's, Burger King or Kentucky Fried Chicken. If you've ever been curious as to which one has more, here is the top 10 in order of number of locations in Dallas:

1. McDonald's
2. Dairy Queen
3. Sonic (doesn't *that* surprise you?)

4. Whataburger
5. Long John Silver's
6. Sandwich Chef
7. Church's Fried Chicken
8. Burger King
9. Pizza Inn (based in Dallas, by the way)
10. Jack-in-the-Box

Of all the restaurant chains in Dallas, no burger house could match Chili's average annual sales per store - $1.3 million.

El Chico, another Dallas tradition, began in 1940 when the Cuellar family opened a little cafe in Kaufman, Texas. Mama cooked and the boys helped. The family moved to Dallas and opened one restaurant, then another and another, and pretty soon they were the largest Mexican food servers in America. The oldest standing El Chico is located in the Lakewood Village on Abrams.

A few years ago the family sold out for about $20 million to Campbell-Taggert. Not long after that, Campbell-Taggert was bought by mega-conglomerate Anheuser-Busch but had to spin off any property which sold alcoholic drinks. El Chico fit into that category and had to be sold before the Anheuser-Busch transaction could take place.

Stepping up to the plate quickly were Gilbert Cuellar (one of the famous "Mama's Boys") and his son, Gilbert Cuellar, Jr., who, together,

*Mrs. Gilbert Cuellar and her son, Gilbert Cuellar, Jr.*

bought the El Chico company back for a reported $12.5 million.

Speaking of El Chico, it was Gilbert Cuellar, Jr. at his Casa Rosa Restaurant in the Inwood Village (site of one of the original and most beloved El Chicos), who - along with Mariano Martinez, of Mariano's in Old Town - introduced sizzling fajitas to Dallas. It has grown to become one of the most popular dishes in the city, but we need to clear up something right here.

Somebody, someplace got the bright idea to put chicken in a flour tortilla and call it a fajita. He is a Dallas man.

The translation of the Mexican word "fajita" into English is "skirt steak," a certain, less-desirable cut of beef. To use the words chicken and fajita in the same phrase is a contradiction in terms. Chicken fajita means "chicken beef."

David Franklin of Dallas' On The Border is the man who has given the world chicken fajitas, and the world seems to appreciate it. The concept is a bonafide home run.

Although it seems like it, not *everybody* is eating chicken fajitas or shrimp fajitas or lobster fajitas. Some people want to eat at the most diverse, more hidden "finds" in town. Well, Dallas, here they are -

**1. Texaco Lunch Box - 3801 Ross at Washington** The best egg rolls in Dallas. Don't let the Texaco gas station facade turn you off.

They don't check your oil or wash your windows
- and they don't even really have any gasoline.
But the food there is a Dallas underground favorite. Everything is "to go."

**2. Theo's Diner - 111 S. Hall Street** Last of the great Dallas diners. Seats about 10. Good food, good service, good clientele. Why we let McDonald's take over these sorts of places will always be a mystery. Not open after lunch.

**3. Gennie's Bishop Grille - 308 N. Bishop** One of the gems of Oak Cliff. Chicken fried steaks, mashed potatoes and all the southern charm Dallas has to offer. If lunch gets crowded there, try its sister restaurant, Rosemarie's at 1411 Zang.

*Prince of Hamburgers on Lemmon Avenue.*

**4. The Prince of Hamburgers - 5200 Lemmon** When was the last time you had a car hop bring a big frosty mug of root beer with your cheeseburger? Well, that's too long. The Prince has an extremely loyal following, but the rest of Dallas can't find it. Keller's is a worthy runner-up, but there is only one Prince.

167

*Escondido's.*

**5. Escondido's - 2210 Butler Street** Looks like it was airlifted from Guadalajara, Mexico, and dropped at the closest vacant lot they could find to Parkland Hospital. Decorated in "early tequila," this place is your best down and dirty Tex-Mex hideaway in Dallas. The bean and cheese nachos are the reason God made beer. It's inexpensive, but never mind - you'll never find it.

*Sonny Bryan's.*

**6. Sonny Bryan's - 2202 Inwood** The most popular hidden barbecue joint in town. It's such a great secret, half the town has already eaten there. The other half can't handle the wait or the grease or the smoke or the lack of tables. Or they don't know about it. Now they do. Eat there or move back to wherever you came from.

*Lakewood Cafe on Abrams.*

7. **Lakewood Cafe - 2111 Abrams** Truck drivers meet there for breakfast, business people eat the lunch hamburgers there and families converge in the evening. All day long individuals will be sipping beers from various corners of the room. This place has character and it has good food. Lakewood fans know about it, but the rest of Dallas needs to discover this wonderful time warp.

*The Mecca on Harry Hines.*

**8. Dunston's Steak House - 5423 W. Lovers Lane** There's nothing hidden about the steak house - and there're *four* other Dunston's in Dallas - but this location has a hidden back room which is as close to a country club setting as you'll find in a Dallas restaurant. Regulars play cards, make oil and gas deals, have a few drinks and head home. Made up, for the most part, of Easy Way refugees, it's a great place to enjoy a good steak. Use the back entrance, if you can find it.

**9. The Mecca - 10422 Harry Hines** Not exactly located on gourmet restaurant row, The Mecca is a southern food legend in this city. The breakfast will change your life, but the lunch favorite - the chicken fried steak - is its most famous dish. People who drive trucks go there. You should, too.

**10. Adair's Saloon - 2624 Commerce** Why is a saloon on this list? Because if you have friends in town who want a Texas dining experience, try Adair's. It's a downhome honky-tonk, features good country music, pool and shuffleboard, and has a hamburger that should win an Academy Award. It's *giant* and goes good with a million beers. Tell your friends all burgers in Texas look and taste like that. It'll make 'em want to relocate to Dallas.

The Second 10 includes, in no particular order, Mia's, Highland Park Pharmacy, Little Gus', Snuffer's, Thailanna, Aw Shucks, Goff's, Highland Park Cafeteria, Celebration, and Bob Willy's. Spanish Village is not on the list because it's *my* personal favorite and is as crowded as I'd like.

All of the hidden restaurants are inexpensive to moderate. If you are tired of the same old food at the same old places, venture outside of your neighborhood and try these hidden Dallas favorites.

If you don't like the idea of straying too far from your home turf and are uncomfortable trying something new, you'll love the restaurant row located on Composite at Walnut Hill and Stemmons Freeway (I-35E). A wonderland of national food chains are lined up - for your convenience - and have ample room for you, your family and half the conventioneers in Dallas.

In order to work up a hearty appetite, how about a round of golf?

You don't have to be a zillionaire to play golf in Dallas. There are plenty of country clubs which provide members with all the golf they can handle. But if you're not a country club kind of person, Dallas has some excellent municipal golf courses:

Stevens Park, 1005 Montclair, 670-7506
Tenison, 3501 Samuel Blvd., 823-5350
LB Houston, 11223 Luna Road, 869-1778
Cedar Crest, 1800 Southerland, 943-1004
Grover Keaton, 2323 N. Jim Miller, 388-4831

*Golf at the Lakewood Country Club.*

Among the suburban municipal and public courses, the best are Firewheel in Garland (494-7136), Bear Creek at the D/FW Airport (453-0140), Mesquite Municipal (270-7457), Plano Municipal (423-5444) and Sherrill Park in Richardson (235-8331).

Rules, rental and prices vary from course to course, but one thing remains the same: you don't have to be wealthy to enjoy a nice round of golf in Dallas.

The sport was introduced to the city in 1896 when three prominent Dallasites built a six-hole course on 30 acres approximately where Lemmon and Oak Lawn intersect. H.L. Edwards, C.E. Wellesley and Richard Potter were the founders of what was then called "The Golfers Club."

The greens were simply small pieces of land, cleared of the grass, brush and weeds. Ordinary tomato cans were sunk as holes and tree branches flagged each of the six holes. To protect the greens from cattle hoofs, wire fences surrounded them.

The first golf tournament ever held in Dallas was in 1898 and was won by J.C. O'Connor, who was presented with a loving cup full of sparkling champagne. Richard Potter was the president of the club at the time.

On January 17, 1900 the club procured a charter from the state and incorporated, selling 320 shares at $25 each. With the $8,000 raised, they bought the land where the six holes were, and the Dallas Golf and Country Club was born.

Incorporators were H.L. Edwards and Robert Ralston. First president was J.T. Trezevant while

Ralston served as vice president and George F. Walker was secretary. Members read like a "Who's Who" of Dallas.

Original stockholders in Dallas' first golf and country club were H.S. Edwards, F.J. Dobson, E.O. Tenison, J.T. Trezevant, Robert Ralston, J.C. O'Connor, J.C. Duke, Charles C. Cobb, L.A. Pires, R. Benby, Royal A. Ferris, C.E. Wellesley, A.H. Belo, Jr., George Sturges, R.N.G. Smith, G.F. Walker, J.B. Oldham, G.B. Dealey, F.J. Baker, R.K. Gaston, E.M. Reardon, T.L. Monagan, Sam P. Cochran, Sam Leake, H.S. Keating, L. Wells Baldwin, Charles L. Dexter, L.S. Smith, Percey E. Ginn, Alex C. Coke, Seth Miller, D.G. Wolfenden, M.A. Shumard and H.A. Hamilton.

In 1911 the club moved a few miles north along Turtle Creek to a spot in Highland Park. The old location was sold for a handsome profit and a new, Elizabethan-inspired clubhouse was built by C.D. Hill at the new location, where the club was (and is) known as the Dallas Country Club. In 1955 a fire burned the impressive structure to the ground and a new, more efficient, but less romantic, clubhouse was built and still stands.

The old land where the golf club originated was developed into what is now part of the Oak Lawn/Turtle Creek area. A colossal university building was built adjacent to the golf club in 1906 by H.A. Overbeck. It was commissioned by Vincentian Fathers and the school was called

Holy Trinity College (across the street from the current Holy Trinity Catholic Church on Oak Lawn). The name was changed to Dallas University in 1910, and the school went bankrupt in the ealry 1940s. Jesuit High School took over the location until the building was demolished in 1963. Jesuit moved to a new campus (out in the country) on Inwood, north of Forest Lane, and the site of the old school is now called Turtle Creek Village, with several high rise and mid-size office buildings and retail outlets.

The Dallas Golf and Country Club was the only place in town to play golf until 1912, when Lakewood Country Club was founded. In 1917 the third course, at Cedar Crest Country Club in Oak Cliff, was organized. Brook Hollow Golf Club was next, in 1920, followed by Glen Haven in 1922. Glen Haven later became known as Glen Lakes, and the course was sold to developers in the mid '70s. The developments along Central Expressway between NorthPark and Walnut Hill are located on the old Glen Lakes golf course.

In 1923 Tenison opened (and had grass greens in 1925) and Bob-o-Links was opened in 1924 by Harry McCommas. It had sand greens until 1938 and it, too, was sold to developers. Now the only visible remainder of the course is the name of Bob-O-Link Drive, running east from Abrams, near the Lakewood Village.

In the 1930s Tenison was known as Hustlers' Park as golfers spent as much time wagering as they did putting. The most famous hustler in Dallas history was Titanic Thompson, who won and lost millions, killed five men, married five women and was known as one of the legendary con-men of the betting world.

One of Thompson's wives, Nora, had been granted a divorce because he was "too dangerous, traveled too much and carried a gun." A few years later Nora married a man called "Pretty Boy" Floyd.

Titanic would play someone $100 a hole for nine holes and complain about his bad luck. In an after-golf poker game he would act as if his emotions had taken over and was betting to get even. When the winner would agree to play him again, this time for $1,000 a hole for 18 holes, he would accept. All money was put up in advance, including over $30,000 in side bets, which he covered for himself. Then the next morning, Titanic, a scratch golfer, would beat the socks off his opponent, pocket the money - up to $56,000 per day - and be gone.

One of the great golf matches of Dallas/Fort Worth history occurred on the day a group of businessmen put Titanic up against a young Fort Worth talent named Byron Nelson. Both men were playing for pride, not money. But behind their backs huge side-bets were being thrown back and forth. When the dust settled, Titanic Thompson had shot a course record 29 on the back nine of the Ridglea Country Club in Fort Worth and had beaten Byron Nelson.

The second greatest hustler in Dallas history was a brash young Mexican boy named Lee Trevino, who would use a Dr. Pepper bottle as his golf clubs and beat the pants off some of Dallas' better golfers at Tenison and Hardie's Pitch and Putt on Lovers Lane and Greenville (now Old Town and the Village Apartments). Trevino, of course, was the one-time caddie who has gone on to become one of the great pro golfers of all time. Trevino never played Titanic in person, but he did outplay Ray Floyd in El Paso several years ago, costing Thompson - who was getting up in his years - $9,000 he had bet on Floyd.

The first recorded tennis games in Dallas took place in 1890, the same year Col. Henry Exall dammed up Turtle Creek to make Exall Lake, along Lakeside Drive. Two tennis courts - one at Dr. Hughes' house on Hughes Circle and the other at Captain Sydney Smith's residence at Fairland - were the only known tennis courts in Dallas until two grass courts were laid out at City Park in 1892, where the Surprise Lawn Tennis Club was formed. The courts were on the site of today's Ambassador Hotel.

The Dallas Lawn Tennis Club was formed in 1908 and built six courts at Lake Cliff Park. By 1909 the board of directors consisted of some of the most influential businessmen of the day, recognizable names such as Eli Sanger, Percy Davis, Sloan Simpson, Laurence Kahn, Leslie Waggoner and Sol Dreyfus.

The first municipal courts were built at Oak Lawn Park (now called Lee Park) on Turtle Creek in 1913 and two years later the first lighted courts were installed.

## Other firsts in Dallas:

### FIRST FOOTBALL GAME - 1891
Dallas versus Tyler. They were the only two teams in Texas at the time. Dallas won. The next year Dallas played a new team, Fort Worth, on Christmas day and won 16-0. The newspapers listed the quarterback as "the one-fourth back."

### FIRST HIGH SCHOOL FOOTBALL TEAM - 1901
Organized by Marion Brinker and George Sargeant, this team was known as "North Dallas."

### FIRST SMU FOOTBALL GAME - 1915
The Mustangs took it on the chin against TCU, 43-0, coming right out of the chute. But if you think *that's* bad, the next year SMU lost to Baylor, 61-0; lost to Texas A&M, 62-0; lost to the University of Texas, 74-0; before finally getting on the scoreboard, losing to Rice 143-3. At least they had a team then.

## FIRST DALLAS BASEBALL TEAM - 1888

The Dallas Eagles won the Texas League pennant in the league's first season, with a record of 55-27. The team was nicknamed "the Hams."

## FIRST TAVERN - 1846

The Dallas Tavern, at the corner of Houston and Commerce.

## FIRST HORSE - 1841

Neshoba, which means Gray Wolf. John Neely Bryan's horse when he rode in and founded the town.

## FIRST AIRSHIP - 1908

The "Aerial Queen" flew into town in April and stayed for two weeks, offering daily flights for interested Dallasites.

## FIRST FEMALE MAYOR - 1987

Annette Strauss. You've come a long way, baby.

## FIRST OUTBOARD MOTORBOAT RACE - 1929

Twelve boats entered this exciting race at White Rock Lake.

## FIRST SHERIFF - 1846

John Huitt. He was a frontier sheriff battling outlaws, misfits and Indians.

## FIRST STREET - c.1840

Preston Road was here before Dallas was. It was the trail John Neely Bryan followed when he came here. It began at Holland Coffee's Trading Post on the Red River (now underwater at Lake Texoma) and followed the watershed line between two rivers to what is now downtown Dallas. It was popular because there were no large rivers or creeks to cross. Today, Preston Road follows that same trail.

*Preston Road existed before Dallas.*

## FIRST CITY PARK - 1880s

City Park, now restored and called Old City Park, just south of downtown.

## FIRST PIPE ORGAN - 1879

World famous organist Gustavus Gursten of Saxony came to Dallas for a concert at St. Matthews Cathedral. He played there because it had the only organ in town.

## FIRST DIVORCE - 1846

Charlotte Dalton sued her husband Joseph for divorce. The jury granted the divorce, then later that day Mrs. Dalton married the foreman of the jury.

## FIRST SHOES - 1843

When John Neely Bryan married Margaret Beeman, she made them each a pair of moccasins. They were the first shoes made in Dallas.

## FIRST FIRE DEPARTMENT - 1871

August of that year, the Dallas Hook and Ladder Company #1 was formed.

## FIRST ART SCHOOL - 1902

It was the first complete art school in all of Texas, founded by Vivian Aunspaugh.

## FIRST HOTEL - 1853

Crutchfield House was the first real hotel in Dallas, located at the northwest corner of Main and Houston. It burned down in 1860, was rebuilt but burned again in 1888. It was not rebuilt again.

## FIRST SCHOOL BUS - 1877

A school wagon began operation on September 6, 1877, taking girls and young ladies to Dallas College (or Rock College) for 30¢ per month.

## FIRST DALLAS SYMPHONY PERFORMANCE - 1900

Under the direction of Hans Kreissig, the DSO first performed on May 22, 1900, at Turner Hall, Harwood and Young Streets. The DSO was made up of 36 members and the performance lost $1,000, which was personally made up for by Kreissig.

## FIRST MARRIAGE LICENSE - 1846

Although John Neely Bryan and Margaret Beeman were the first Dallasites to be married, Crawford Trees and Anna Kimmel were the first to apply for a marriage license in Dallas. Bryan and his bride had to be married at Bonham because nobody in Dallas could perform the marriage.

## FIRST LAWYER - 1845
John McCoy was the first lawyer in town. Second was John M. Crockett and third was Nat M. Burford.

## FIRST MOTION PICTURE - 1897
Scenes from a Mexican duel, a lynching, and Niagara Falls were included in an exhibition of "Edison's newest invention - the Vitascope," seen at the Dallas Opera House.

## FIRST ICE HOCKEY GAME - 1941
On October 1 of 1941, hockey was played on ice for the first time in Dallas.

## FIRST CAR SALESMAN - 1900
Henry "Dad" Garrett bought the first car in Dallas from E.H.R. Green and sold it to somebody else. He stayed in the car business.

## FIRST BRANDS - 1846
Cattle marks and brands were first recorded by John Beeman, John Neely Bryan, W.P. Carder and John Young in September, 1846.

## FIRST BILL OF SALE - 1846
A slave woman was actually the first bill of sale recorded in Dallas, on March 17, 1846. Edward Welborn was the seller and John Young was the buyer.

## FIRST DOCTOR - 1842
Dr. Calder was the town's first physician. He was killed a few months later by Indians in Collin County.

## FIRST DALLAS HIGH SCHOOL TO WIN A STATE CHAMPIONSHIP - 1924
Oak Cliff High was the state champion in football in 1924.

## FIRST MODEL T FORD - 1906
W.W. Adair was the proud owner of Dallas' first Model T Ford.

## FIRST COURTHOUSE - 1842
John Neely Bryan's cabin was the first courthouse in Dallas.

## FIRST MAYOR - 1856
Dr. Samuel Pryor was the city's first mayor.

## FIRST NEWSPAPER - 1849
James Wellington "Weck" Latimer published the *Cedar Snag* in 1849. It was later renamed the *Dallas Herald* (not related to today's *Dallas Times Herald*.)

## FIRST WOMEN ON THE SCHOOL BOARD - 1908
When Mrs. E.P. Turner and Mrs. T.T. Tucker

began their historic roles as the first female school board members, one disgruntled board member said, "Women are biologically disqualified. The efficiency and the businesslike dispatch of the board will be hampered."

## FIRST FAIR - 1859

At the corner of Preston and Commerce, on the western edge of the city, a fair was sponsored by the Dallas Agricultural and Mechanical Association.

## FIRST POWER PLANT - 1882

Built by private capital at the corner of Austin and Ross, this plant served Dallas' first electrical customers - the local saloons, including Mayer's Garden on Elm and Ervay. There were a total of six lights, but they lit up the town.

## FIRST CATHOLIC SERVICE - 1859

Conducted by the Reverend Sebastian Augagneur of Nacogdoches, it was held in the home of Maxime Guillot during the summer of 1859.

## FIRST PRO FOOTBALL TEAM - 1952

The Dallas Texans of the NFL lasted one season here, then went on to Baltimore, where, as the Colts, they won the first sudden death playoff victory in NFL history. They defeated the New York Giants 23-17, in 1958, to win the world championship. They are now the Indianapolis Colts.

## FIRST DISTRICT JUDGE - 1846
The Sixth District Court, with William B. Ochiltree as circuit judge, was brought to Dallas in 1846. The first Dallas grand jury returned 61 indictments that year: 51 gambling, 4 assault and battery, 1 murder and 1 challenge to a duel.

## FIRST MANUFACTURING PLANT - 1850
Maxime Guillot opened a wagon shop at Elm and Houston in 1850.

## FIRST TELEPHONE - 1881
Installed "as an experiment" in 1881, Dallas' first telephone line ran between the Browder Springs (Old City Park) Pumping Station to its office at Main and Harwood, to the downtown fire station. It was to be used to tell the plant where to pump water in the event of a fire. A sub-line from this system ran from Philip Sanger's mansion in the Cedars to the Sanger Brothers department store. Col. A.H. Belo, while he was living in Galveston, had already purchased the first telephone in Texas.

## FIRST HIGH RISE BUILDING - 1888
The North Texas Building, on Main between Lamar and Poydras, lost its first tenant to the Crash of '93. It was finally destroyed in 1967 to make

way for the proposed Two Main Place.

## FIRST VIADUCT - 1912
Now called the Houston Street Viaduct, it was called the Oak Cliff Viaduct in 1912. At the time it was the longest reinforced concrete bridge in the world.

*Barbeque under the Houston Street Viaduct.*

*Old Sanger Brothers Building, now El Centro College.*

## FIRST COMMUNITY COLLEGE - 1966
El Centro was the first college in the Dallas
County Community College District when it
opened in the old Sanger Brothers Building in
1966.

## FIRST HOT AIR BALLOON FLIGHT - 1861

Newspaper accounts of Professor Wallace's rides offered to Dallasites in April of 1861 said, "This aerial navigator will furnish a through ticket to the other side of the Jordan to anyone who wishes to make the trip with him into parts unknown."

## FIRST CHURCH - 1845

On May 1, 1845, several men and women met at Isaac Webb's house to form a church. The first camp meeting was held that fall. Daniel Shook was the circuit rider. In 1846, the first church building was erected - a log house (18'x18') called Webb's Chapel - two miles west of Farmers Branch. Later, part of this congregation teamed up to form Cochran's Chapel (still located at Northwest Highway and Midway). In May of 1846 the first Baptist church, Union Chapel, was formed in Dallas. The first Christian church was formed that year in Horde's Ridge (now called Oak Cliff.)

## FIRST JUNIOR IN COLLEGE TO WIN THE HEISMAN TROPHY - 1948

Doak Walker of SMU received 1,221 votes while the runner-up got 443 votes, in one of the great runaway Heisman victories.

## FIRST BOWLING ALLEY - 1847
An open-air bowling alley was opened in Cedar Springs in 1847.

*First airmail delivery of the Dallas Times Herald.*

## FIRST AERIAL PHOTO OF DALLAS - 1913
Taken by Frank Rogers, *Dallas Times Herald* photographer.

## FIRST DALLAS SCHOOLS SUPERINTENDENT - 1884
W.A. Boles was the first Dallas Schools Superintendent in 1884.

## FIRST BARBED WIRE - 1872
John Campbell of Richardson got his wire off the first TH&C train that came to town.

## FIRST THEATER - 1873
Field Opera House, the first legitimate theater in Dallas, was built by J.Y. and Tom Field, and was leased to Capt. William Crisp for its first season. It was later renamed Dallas Opera House.

## FIRST SHOPPING CENTER - 1931
Highland Park Shopping Village was one of the first two planned, off-street shopping centers in America. It was the prototype for the modern suburban shopping center.

## FIRST DISTILLERY - 1850
Gold and Donaldson set up a distillery in Cedar Springs, selling whiskey at 15¢ a quart or 50¢ a gallon. It was the best whiskey in Dallas County for years.

## FIRST PAVED STREETS - 1884
Elm and Main were paved with bois d'arc blocks from the Trinity Riverbottoms at Seagoville.

## FIRST NIGHT FOOTBALL GAME - 1930
That fall, 45,000 fans crammed into the Cotton Bowl to see the first game played under lights in Dallas. North Dallas beat Sunset, 7-6.

## FIRST BICYCLE - 1876

Hugh Blakeney's bike had wooden wheels - a large one in the front and a small trailer wheel on the back. It had iron tires. Six years later Gross Scruggs paid $162.50 for the first rubber-tired bicycle in town.

## FIRST SAXOPHONE - 1883

In August of 1883, a saxophone was played at Mayer's Garden. A published review called it "an instrument which gave forth exquisite music, like the human voice."

## FIRST DOG - 1841

Tubby was John Neely Bryan's bear-dog who came with him to the Trinity. The dog's name came from the Choctaw name - Tubbee, meaning "killer."

## FIRST LONELY HEARTS CLUB - 1882

The Texas Marriage Aid Association sold shares for $5 each and shareholders were paid 50¢ per day until he or she found a mate. Many leading citizens participated.

## FIRST FERRY BOAT - 1842

John Neely Bryan built a boat out of two large cottonwood logs, dug out like canoes and fastened together with puncheons. Buffalo hair was twisted into the needed rope. It was docked right where the Commerce Street viaduct is today.

## FIRST CITY MANAGER - 1931
When Dallas voted to use the city council/city manager form of government, John N. Edy was selected as the first city manager.

## FIRST POST OFFICE - 1842
John Neely Bryan's cabin was the first Dallas post office.

## FIRST AUTOMOBILE - 1899
Col. E.H.R. Green's two cylinder, two seat "St. Louis" was the first car in Texas. He drove it from Terrell to Dallas in a little over five hours.

## FIRST AUTO RACE - 1905
The first 100-mile auto race ever held in the United States took place at Fair Park. Two Franklins, a Peerless, a Columbia and a Pope-Toledo entered, and the winner was the Pope-Toledo, owned by none other than E.H.R. Green, and driven by Green's chauffeur, Ollie Savin.

## FIRST BRICK VENEER HOUSE - 1885
Mrs. William Gregg Randall had the first brick home in Dallas built at the corner of St. Paul and Munger.

*Tom Gooch, great-grandson of Martha Gilbert*

## FIRST WOMAN - 1842
Martha Gilbert, wife of Capt. Mabel Gilbert, was the first woman to live in Dallas. Exactly 100 years later her great grandson, Tom Gooch, became the publisher of the *Dallas Times Herald*, in 1942.

## FIRST CHILD BORN IN DALLAS - 1843
The first anglo girl born in Dallas County was Alice West Floyd.

## FIRST JUNIOR BASEBALL LEAGUE - 1913

Founded by Wally Moore and Ty Catron, little baseball hit Dallas in 1913.

## FIRST MOTORCYCLE - 1907

Officially registered as Dallas' 295th vehicle, it belonged to A.S. Millican.

## FIRST LAND PATENT - 1842

John Grigsby was granted Dallas' first land patent on January 28, 1842, by the President of the Republic of Texas, Sam Houston.

## FIRST WILL - 1846

On July 23 of that year, J.A. Simmons recorded the first will in Dallas.

## FIRST STRIKE - 1884

That summer the railway workers went on strike in Dallas.

## FIRST GRIST MILL - 1846

Aaron Overton and his sons, C.C. and Perry, built Dallas' first grist mill, which had a capacity of 100 bushels of wheat a day.

*Dallas Hall at SMU, 191*

# WHAT YOU DIDN'T KNOW ABOUT

**Southern Methodist University**

The founding of SMU is a long, interesting tale, beginning back in 1911, when it was chartered. There was much discussion about whether the Methodists would start a whole new school in Dallas or would move Southwestern University out of Georgetown to Big D, then the 60th largest city in America.

When it was decided to start a new school, the biggest proponent of the Dallas location was Dr. Robert H. Hyer, the president of Southwestern. When SMU opened, Dr. Hyer was its first president and while Dallas celebrated this new university, he was being hanged in effigy in Georgetown.

On April 13, 1911, the new school was named Texas Wesleyan University. Some of the folks here in town who put up the land and money - $300,000 cash, 133 original acres (donated by Mrs. John S. Armstrong), another 153.5 adjoining acres and half interest in another 722 acres of Caruth land - didn't like the name at all. The next day a new name was given the school, Southern Methodist University.

Dr. Hyer, the father of the school, actually wanted to call it the University of Dallas. He gave a speech to the Dallas Chamber of Commerce about what he'd like the school to be and what he'd like to call it, then the very next week, a small little Catholic college, Holy Trinity College (now the site of Turtle Creek Village) reapplied for a state charter under the name, "The University of Dallas."

Said Dr. Hyer's daughter, Margaret Hyer Thomas, "Someone in that audience was a loyal Catholic."

Dr. Hyer picked the school colors, red for Harvard and blue for Yale. He hired the same firm which designed Stanford Unirersity to lay out the campus, and on opening day, in the fall of 1911, 706 students registered, one of the two largest opening enrollments of any university in the history of the United States.

## The Sportatorium

There's no way to explain it except to come right out and say it. The Sportatorium has the coldest beer in Dallas. Each brew ($1.25) is kept in ice-cold vaults and, due to Sportatorium rules, must be poured from the can into a cup.

Most Texans agree that there is a big difference between cold beer and ice-cold beer. World Class Championship Wrestling, on Friday nights, features the latter, at the Sportatorium.

*Wrestling fans enjoy ice cold beer at the Sportatorium.*

*Campisi's Egyptian Lounge.*

## Campisi's

The most natural question in all of Dallas is, "Why does a restaurant called the Egyptian Lounge serve some of the best Italian food in town?"

It is baffling, but there is a reason. When the Campisi family took over the location years ago, the former tenant was a restaurant called the Egyptian Lounge. The Campisi family, a little tight on start-up capital, went ahead and left the sign up and called themselves the Egyptian Lounge. They then started serving some of the best pizza you'll find in Dallas.

It has continued to be known by both names and its popularity grows each year. And it has Dallas' best line to stand in. One hasn't experienced Dallas until one has been to Campisi's, on Mockingbird Lane.

## Loop 12

One of Dallas' most important roadways, Loop 12 is known by various names as it winds completely around the city. In Oak Cliff it is known as Ledbetter, in East Dallas it's called Buckner Boulevard and in West Dallas, Loop 12 is known as Walton Walker.

Running through North Dallas, Loop 12 has been given the very unimaginative name of Northwest Highway.

## Jim Wright

The current Speaker of the House is known throughout the nation as a Fort Worth man - which he is - but he was raised in Dallas, where he graduated from Adamson High School in Oak Cliff.

## Big Tex

It's hard to believe, but Big Tex was originally Santa Claus.

He was made in Kerens, Texas, just south of Dallas and was purchased in 1951 for $750 by Bob Thornton. He made his debut as Big Tex, (wearing a sombrero!) at the 1952 State Fair of Texas. He had to have a little plastic surgery done on his face because he cheeks were a little too pink for Big Tex.

He has stood - all 52 feet of him - at every State Fair of Texas since 1952, clad in his massive H.D. Lee attire. He continues to greet fairgoers with his familiar "How-dy Folks!" in a Texas drawl now over 35 years old.

*The Texas Kid.*

## The Texas Kid

Willard Watson, known by most people as the Texas Kid, is one of the more creative minds in Dallas. He has been discovered by the city's art community, but few people outside of his neighborhood have experienced Watson's front yard, which is one of the most incredible sights you'll see in Dallas.

It's better than a museum and is tucked away in a quiet neighborhood just east of Love Field, at 6614 Kenwell, between University and Mockingbird.

The Kid and his yard art personify *Hidden Dallas* more than anything else you'll see, hear or feel in Dallas, Texas.

## Photo credits

The Dallas Public Library -
*iv,viii,3,9,20,21,60,62,63,67,88,93,98,100,102,109,111,112,*
*113,115,140,143,145,148,149,176,177,192,194,198,200.*
Ron Evans -
*ii,iii,x,1,11,12,28,29,33,34,50,51,65,69,70,71,72,76,78,81,84,*
*87,88,91,94,96,107,110,116,122,126,132,160,164,166,167,*
*168,169,170,171,174,184,191,204,209,210.*
Royce Blankenship -
*119,123,124,125,130,135,136,138.*
Southland Corporation -
*22,23,154,156,157.*
Ed Thompson -
*38.*
NorthPark -
*24,25,41,42,43,45,48.*
Texas Instruments -
*55,56,57,59.*
Baylor Medical Center -
*97.*